To VLBK, the sweetest part of my life since our first date on Halloween 1946: A buoy, a cheerleader, my best friend, and greatest love.

Contents

Most English teachers for the past forty years have highly valued the little book written by William Strunk, Jr. and revised by E. B. White (1959). Many of us who prize the written word still value and use *The Elements of Style*. White was a student of Professor Strunk at Cornell in Ithaca, New York, in 1919, and they became lifelong friends. The most precious part of the book to me has always been the short paragraph Strunk wrote about one of his favorite topics. White said that, in sixty-three words, here was an essay on the nature of brevity that could change the world.

I follow with the essence of Strunk's wonderful little essay by paring it even more, because *quality is always improvable:*

> Good writing is concise. A sentence has no unnecessary words, a paragraph no unnecessary sentences, for the same reason a drawing has no unnecessary lines, a machine no unnecessary parts. This requires not that the writer create only short sentences, avoid all detail, and treat subjects only in outline, but that *every word tell.*

My book, too, is partly about brevity because I believe that when writers want readers to value a proposal, they cut to the chase. Johann Goethe, the great German writer and thinker, said that trial and error is the best way to learn because by trying and failing and repeating the process until one finds success, you eliminate the chaff from the wheat, throw the former away, and use the latter for gain and growth. My point is that this treatise is short and to the point. The reader who subscribes to its assertions may use it as a handbook to make changes for positive student growth.

What is the handbook about? The bottom line is how to cause almost every, if not every, student to graduate from high school competent or better in relevant subject matter and be responsible in citizenship. To accomplish that, however, we must people our schools with a plethora of STARs (successful and responsible teachers). Because I've worked with myriad such pedagogues, I know what they look like and how they behave; thus, the first few chapters address successful teachers' specifications. However, teachers do not become successful in a few years. It takes a while.

Successful teachers must also have the proper conditions to succeed, so the later chapters deal with those conditions or assumptions:

1. The successful teachers mentor those who are on the road to success.
2. School and central office leaders practice STAR Theory (see chapter 1 for the definition of the theory).
3. Students attend school regularly.
4. Schools are small.
5. Students who pose a danger to others are placed in alternative settings.
6. Time-out rooms replace in-school suspension rooms.
7. Except for students who pose a danger to others, teachers work with all student transgressions using natural/logical consequences.
8. Teachers, administrators, and board members embrace and support STAR Theory.
9. Adults working directly with students treat the district and their own schools' missions as constitutions.
10. At least two-thirds of the community stakeholders treat the district mission and their respective school missions as constitutions.

No way exists for virtually all youngsters to exit school at least competent in relevant subject matter and responsible in citizenship without districts deciding to meet those conditions. I present my case mainly with two kinds of evidence—authority and documentation. The third kind of evidence, personal experience, does not make its way into this book often, but every district has enough experts—that is, authoritative experience—to make the STAR Theory work. Therefore, every school district in the country is able to take the ideas in this book and turn out the kinds of students our critics have said we do not produce. Our critics have been correct; we do not produce enough competent, quality, and responsible youngsters. But, if these critics truly want what they say they want, they must be willing to help make the prescription outlined a reality. Without meeting the ten assumptions listed earlier, and without attracting, developing, and supporting the STARs needed to do this, we are destined to mediocrity. Who wants that?

CHAPTER 1

Foundation for a Stairway to the Stars

A theory is an idea the originator wants people to test in practice until the idea (theory) becomes virtually unimpeachable. When the apple fell on Newton's head, or so the story goes, he asked why. Consequently, Sir Isaac developed theories that, through successful testing in life, resulted in what is known as the *laws* (virtually unimpeachable) *of gravity*. That is a law of physical science. STAR (Successful Teachers Are Real) Theory resides in another domain, social science.

It is more difficult to replicate the successful practice of social science theory than of physical science theory because the former often deals with the gamut of human emotions, intellect, and physiognomy; the latter works with more controllable, inanimate things. However, many social science theories have eventually reached, or have come close to, invincibility. As an example, because of its positive results, Pygmalion Theory, more commonly known today as the *Self-Fulfilling Prophesy,* has become so popular that most educational leaders are constantly looking for pedagogues who use this theory to enhance the confidence and the achievement of their students. The origin of Pygmalion Theory is found in Greek mythology: Pygmalion was a king who also was a sculptor. In a major project, he was sculpting a beautiful maiden out of marble, a marble lady he named *Galatea.* While working, he fell in love with Galatea and wished mightily for her to be real. The queen of the goddesses caused it to happen, and Pygmalion married Galatea. A beautiful painting called *Pygmalion and Galatea* hangs in the Metropolitan Museum of Art in New York City. No more appropriate story could precede what comes next, for successful teachers, above all, believe in the inevitability of the success of all their students.

That leads to the thesis of this treatise, *STAR Theory:*

Sound in pedagogy, the successful teacher creates and maintains a caring relationship with all students, rejects their acts and expressions of irresponsibility and teaches them responsibility. Ultimately, almost all, if not all, the successful teacher's charges exit competent or better in relevant subject matter and responsible in citizenship.

Pedagogues falling short of this often are okay teachers, but unless they are at one with the thesis, they are not successful, and successful teachers are the STARs of every school. Actually, when more than half who teach in a school, district, or nation reach success, it is almost certain that violence in that school, district, or nation plummets to unheard-of lows. This is more than a by-product of STAR Theory; it is a direct result of it, and thus illustrates the importance of successful teaching. We discuss this assertion in later chapters when we relate how schools, districts, and communities address the assumptions implicit in STAR Theory. For now, however, examining the affective part of the theory (creating and maintaining a caring relationship with all students) is necessary at the outset. Many teachers excel in pedagogy, but if they do not create and maintain a caring relationship with all students, they fall far short in teaching all students consistently responsible behavior.

What are the requirements for the affective part of STAR Theory? According to Carl Rogers in his book *Freedom to Learn* (1969), three teacher characteristics affect student learning and citizenship behavior positively. The first is *genuineness/realness*, and it is vital. Otherwise, the teacher loses credibility, the game is over, and both the students and the teacher lose. A wonderfully magical passage in *The Velveteen Rabbit* (Williams 1981) illustrates the point, and readers might wish to refer to it.

However, in human lives real people are straight shooters who do not change demeanor to suit the situation or the company they are in. A genuine person's behavior is predictable when ethics and morality are at stake. Genuineness, however, is not always hard-hitting. A person can be real, yet level with another human being in a kind way to soften a blow when the truth hurts. For instance, when a youngster misbehaves, acts irresponsibly, or expresses irresponsibility, the real teacher kindly points out the problem and teaches a responsible behavior or expression.

For example, a youngster might say, "I wish Jimmy were dead!"

The real teacher's response could be, "If Jimmy were dead, you could not help him become better, could you? Now, how can you help make him better?"

Discussing ways to help the youngster express more responsibility, the teacher and student eventually arrive at a mutual solution, such as, "I wish Jimmy wouldn't be like that. Maybe I can help him change by showing him that I am his friend. I think I'll share some of my lunch with him. He always seems to like the cookies Mom puts in my lunch bag, so today I'm going to offer him one." In a later chapter on discipline, we introduce the concept of class meetings, a tool used by teachers to enhance the teaching of student responsibility by using all the youngsters in the classroom setting.

The genuine teacher's behavior does not shock students. The teacher, for instance, is hardly ever accused of playing favorites because when the facts are available to everyone, it is apparent that the genuine teacher treats each youngster kindly—yet firmly when the occasion requires firmness. The preceding example illustrates this in that the genuine teacher follows up firmly, yet kindly, by helping the student consider alternatives to "I wish Jimmy were dead!" Another common example teaching a responsible act in place of an irresponsible one is pointing out that not coming to school regularly is unacceptable. The teacher calls the irregular-attending youngster aside at an unembarrassing and appropriate time, and asks why this is happening. If an acceptable reason is not forthcoming, the real teacher says, "I'm going to call you at home every morning before school until you attend twenty consecutive school days. Then I'll stop calling to see if that has helped you get here regularly." The real teacher then follows through with compliments when the youngster makes strides toward attending school daily.

Many young people can read a phony adult a mile away because youngsters tend to operate from a foundation of genuineness. Some adults, however, are uncannily clever, and sadly, they fool the young for a while. When the youngsters discover the adults they trusted are not genuine, the results often are devastating to the youngsters. So, one sees easily why the quality of realness or genuineness is essential to success in teaching. In the end, genuine teachers tend to produce genuine students much more often than not, and they do so through modeling genuineness/realness.

An important message for a teacher to internalize is to be oneself. It is all right to emulate the qualities of those you admire, but do not try to be those people. You are only real when you know who you *are* and behave that way.

Genuineness/realness is described no more nobly, concisely, and accurately than in a sentence Ralph Waldo Emerson wrote in his remarkable essay *Self-Reliance* (1949). Many scholars believe this sentence is one of the finest in the English language (Williams 1956): "It is easy in the world to live after the world's opinion; it is easy in solitude to live after our own; but the great man is he who in the midst of the crowd keeps with perfect sweetness the independence of solitude." With the changing in the sentence of *man* to *person* and *he* to *one,* Emerson's beautiful thought is free of the sexist language peculiar to the nineteenth century, and even to today's. Thus changed, the sentence is ready for placement above prominent school portals for emulation.

The second essential successful teacher characteristic is exhibiting unconditional positive regard for all students, regardless of their periodic transgressions. That's not always an easy task. A poignant example, extreme as it is, comes also from fictional literature:

In Victor Hugo's *Les Miserables* (1908), the protagonist, Jean val Jean, is paroled after many years in prison for stealing a loaf of bread to feed his sister and her child who were starving during an economic depression in France. Because Jean cannot find work, he breaks parole by leaving the province. His antagonist, Javert, who is a member of the police, pursues Jean relentlessly for years, only to find him greatly reformed and the mayor of his community. Although Javert has always had a strong belief in bringing to justice those who break the law, he cannot force himself to arrest Jean val Jean because of Jean's remarkable transformation, community service, and leadership. Instead of returning Jean to prison, Javert's new unconditional positive regard for his nemesis causes him to . . . well, read Hugo's memorable novel to find out. No sensitive person reveals the denouement of a great book. There is one section in the novel called "The Bishop's Candlesticks," by which only the world's most unemotional people are not moved. It is a quite different example of unconditional positive regard that readers marvel at when reading about the Bishop and Jean val Jean. At least the one-act play, *The Bishop's Candlesticks*, should be required reading in all college and university schools of education. Find and read it if you have not already read the whole book.

The important point related to this characteristic, however, is that successful teachers consistently exhibit unconditional positive regard for all students, especially after rejecting their acts and expressions of irresponsibility then teaching them responsibility. Do not misunderstand. Consequences exist for aberrant student behavior, and successful teachers apply natural/logical consequences while continuing to care for and about the miscreant as well as the mischievous.

The third essential successful teacher characteristic is *high empathy,* or feeling as students feel. Teachers who do not remember how it was to be five, ten, fifteen, or eighteen years old are destined to failure. Unless teachers possess and show high empathy with the youngsters they teach and befriend, they never get to know the students. And knowing them leads to understanding them, which is pivotal in finding the keys to the individual's learning mystique and motivation.

This does not imply that teachers act younger than their ages; it means they remember how it was to be their students' ages, which makes it much easier to understand the reasons for their students' behavior, and what pushes their buttons. Teachers who possess high empathy have much more patience with their students, a requirement for success. More about understanding students and their motivations later.

Again, the three successful teacher characteristics that enhance student achievement and citizenship, according to Rogers (1969), are (1) genuineness/realness, (2) unconditional positive regard for all students, and (3) high empathy. Although Rogers referred to results in students when their teachers exhibit these traits consistently, one might confidently conclude that all adults who possess and exhibit these traits cause good things to happen when they relate to the young—especially when they develop and maintain caring relationships with them while rejecting the youngsters' acts and expressions of irresponsibility and go on to teach them how to behave responsibly. Parents can learn much by reading about and practicing these three characteristics.

This is not a new idea. Glasser (1965), who developed Reality Therapy by working successfully with some of the toughest girls in a California Reformatory many years ago, uses it as a key concept and therapist behavior in treating patients. The idea also pervades virtually all his more recent books, because after he developed Reality Therapy, he turned to education and has been one of this nation's leading educational thinkers and reformers for the past three decades. Some of his more recent books are *The Quality School* (1992), *The Quality School Teacher* (1993), and *Choice Theory* (1998). One more that could help America's plight with broken marriages is his *Staying Together* (1995). In that book, Glasser offers invaluable help to couples with marital problems, and to those considering marriage. If all U.S. high school seniors read this before graduation, perhaps the country's divorce rate would lessen considerably.

Like W. Edwards Deming, another great visionary who seemed to cry in the wilderness, Glasser, now in his mid-seventies, continues to work with schools trying to convince educators and the public not only that all students *can* learn, but also all students *do* learn when presented the appropriate circumstances and the right educators.

CONCLUSION

STAR Theory emanates from the mind and experiences of a practitioner who has labored in the teaching vineyards for fifty years, from one who has had more than 20,000 students and 2,000 fellow teachers grace his presence, and who has verified every word and thought in STAR Theory and its assumptions. The remainder of this book offers a solution to the problems that have plagued schools, not just since the drop in scores on the SAT, but since their inception. The solution does not point a finger at society, parents, teachers, the young, or at anyone else as the culprits. The solution is simply what is possible to accomplish with people working together to meet the assumptions of STAR (Successful Teachers Are Real) Theory.

Again, this theory is simply stated in two words, STAR Theory, because the STARs of every school are the successful teachers who inhabit the environs. The principals, secretaries, custodians, food service personnel, and all the other people employed by the school district exist, above all, to help the STARs shine more brightly. That includes the superintendent and even the members of the board of education. Why? Because if all these folks do everything within their power to help the STARs (successful teachers) shine more brightly, the students are the winners. And that is why schools exist: to make all students at least competent in relevant subject matter and responsible in citizenship.

However, the people of a school district must work together to make this happen. I read the following on the Associated Press wire years ago when I was working part-time at a radio station supplementing my modest yearly teacher's salary of $3,516. The radio job paid $1.50 an hour, which helped significantly in 1951. I tore the following off the wire and have kept it almost fifty years. It sums up the value of working together:

COOPERATION CAN SOLVE MANY A PROBLEM. JUST THINK, FRECKLES
COULD MAKE A COAT OF TAN IF THEY COULD JUST GET TOGETHER.

The remainder of this book consists of a design for painting a coat
of tan on this nation's schoolhouses, their residents, and the people
who live in the neighborhoods. The next chapter proceeds from the
affective portion of STAR Theory described in this chapter to the theory's powerful introductory words, "Sound in pedagogy . . ." Because
pedagogy is a study that requires years to master, more than one chapter relates to this vital subject. However, while reading, keep in mind
that the artful implementation of pedagogy without developing and
maintaining a caring relationship with all students is an oxymoron.

CHAPTER 2

Sound in Pedagogy

Pedagogy is the art and science of teaching, so a person who is sound in pedagogy is capable of teaching students effectively if certain conditions are present. The introduction and table of contents enumerated the ten assumptions (conditions) of this book's thesis. Later chapters contain these and other ideas I suggest to set the stage for successful teaching. However, no matter how effectively they develop and maintain caring relationships (chapter 1), unless teachers know how and want to teach well, youngsters fail to get what they deserve, a good education. Thus, the challenge to schools of education is to be certain that all students who exit with licensure and professorial recommendations are competent to select relevant subject matter, and to teach it well to students. Further, make certain they want to teach all students assigned to them.

The first requirement for effective teaching (sound pedagogy) is for the teacher to develop a vision or aim. Often, those preparing people to teach the young spend little or no time on this primary ingredient. Successful teaching is like a voyage to a special place. The destination is important, but one's accomplishments en route are more important. No better metaphor exists for this point than the following poem by Constantine Cavafy:

> *Ithaca*
> When you set out on the voyage to Ithaca,
> pray that your journey may be long,
> full of adventure, full of knowledge.
> Of the Laestrygones and the Cyclopes
> and of furious Poseidon, do not be afraid,
> For such on your journey you shall never meet
> if your thoughts remain lofty, if a select

emotion imbues your spirit and your body.
The Laestrygones and the Cyclopes and furious
Poseidon you will never meet unless you
drag them with you in your soul, unless your
soul raises them up before you.

Pray that your journey may be long, that many
may those mornings be when with what
pleasure, with what untold delight you enter
harbors for the first time seen; that you stop
at the Phoenician market places to procure
the goodly merchandise, mother of pearl and
coral, amber and ebony, and voluptuous
perfumes of every kind, as lavish an amount
of voluptuous perfumes as you can; that you
venture on to many Egyptian cities to learn
and yet learn again from the sages.

But, you must always keep Ithaca in mind,
The arrival there is your predestination.
Yet, do not by any means hasten your voyage.
Let it endure for many years, until grown old at
length you anchor at your island rich with all
you have acquired on the way, having never
expected Ithaca would give you riches.

Ithaca has given you the lovely voyage,
Without her you would not have ventured that way.
She has nothing more to give you now.

Poor though you may find her, Ithaca has not
deceived you.
Now that you have become so wise, so full of
experience, you will have understood the
meaning of an Ithaca.

Ithaca is an aim, a vision, and almost all successful people have them.
When they have completed the voyage, however, their decisions and
actions en route have made them who they are. Cavafy's poem has the
ingredients of a real-life voyage today, one filled with adventure and
knowledge. Too, if one keeps thoughts lofty and imbues the body and
spirit with positive emotions, in all probability, the denying forces
might be formidable, but not invincible.

He goes on to write about the excitement of entering harbors one has never seen. Surely this also identifies a successful teacher's continuing desire to broaden experiences, to see, do, and procure things that enhance one's quality of life (mother of pearl, coral, amber, ebony, and voluptuous perfumes of every kind) and increase teaching effectiveness with youngsters.

Venturing to selected Egyptian cities to learn and yet to learn again from the sages is one of the myriad ways teachers grow, also, by learning from sagacious mentors who abound in schools but must be sought and wooed to help the, as yet, less than wise.

The poem's closing lines give heart to those with challenging visions: "Now that you have become so wise, so full of experience, you will have understood the meaning of an Ithaca." Without a powerful vision or aim, one does not become what one is capable of becoming. Thus, the aim or vision is a necessity, but the voyage determines who we really are, who we really become.

A successful teacher has a vision or aim she yearns to reach. On her voyage to realize her destination, she grows in myriad ways by creating small, reachable missions. One of these missions might be to continue her formal education through the master's, the specialist, even the doctorate; another mission might be to read the literature that strengthens her teaching skills, the literature that attracts wholesome people and ideas as she continues growing; and still another is to find a mentor to guide and help her avoid detours that slow her progress. These are just three small, but inevitable missions for the wise pursuer of teaching excellence. If wise, she finds many other continuing missions as she ventures toward Ithaca.

Laurie Beth Jones's (1997) succinct, but pithy article about the vitality of setting and continually revising a personal life mission can be helpful. Jones wrote that if success is measured by accomplishments, creating a mission statement is a time and thought organizer, a way to get what one wants. She wrote that it can change the way one looks at everything. A clear mission statement gives purpose to initiate, evaluate, and refine activities, forcing a re-examination of who one is and what one is about. She cited the preamble to the U.S. Constitution's mission "to create a more perfect union . . ." as our founders outlined the goals and aspirations of a new nation. She also emphasized the importance of a short, to-the-point mission statement that one actually uses daily.

Any mission worth its salt comes to the front of the mind when one is ready to use it. For instance, here are my various mission statements at this stage. Keep in mind that each has changed through the years, but all are short enough to retrieve for the occasion warranted by the circumstances. However, the life mission is always front and center, even when working with or thinking about family and friends, teaching, speaking, writing, reading, or listening. When I have anchored at my island, I hope I will be rich with all I have acquired on the way, not in terms of financial wealth, but in terms of who I am, what I have become. Here then are my mission statements:

Life: Find Garcia[1]; bring out everyone's noblest parts; ponder, view, converse, read, write *selectively*; enjoy living, and be amenable to change.
Teaching: Listen to, take seriously, affirm as significant, and improve the economic well-being and quality of life of all my students.
Family: Demonstrate love often through actions and words.
Friends: Accept unconditionally, serve faithfully, and consider most people my friends.
Speaking: Enrich each listener and stop before most want me to.
Writing: Use in an exemplary manner the six Cs of good writing. (In order of importance, these are content, clarity, conciseness, creativity, cogency, and correctness.)
Reading: Note and use the valuable.
Listening: Record and use the valuable, and let your source know.

Successful teachers are not one dimensional, so they have missions to suit the occasion. For instance, my students know my teaching mission at the first class session. I ask them to copy it then tell me at appropriate times if I am not behaving as the mission reads.

As an example, here is a teacher who tells students that she wants to listen to, take seriously, and affirm each as significant (the first part of this teaching mission). A student finds the teacher slipping up, tells her, and the teacher remedies the situation. That teacher establishes credibility, which leads to trust between the two. This trust is a result of the teacher empowering each student to take part in learning, not only by doing what is asked, but by questioning what is asked if the student is not listened to, taken seriously, and affirmed as significant. The trust that empowerment helps build produces nothing but good things in and out of a classroom.

Subject matter choice is not the issue with the first part of the mission because it deals personally with each student when the teacher interacts with, fails to interact with, responds to, fails to respond to, attends to, or fails to attend to during class and with homework assignments. Similarly, this part of the mission implies listening to, taking seriously, and affirming as significant each member of the learning team—that is, the parents and the principal as well as the students.

The second part of the mission, improve the economic well-being, also leads to students questioning the relevance of some subject matter if the teacher fails to set the stage properly before teaching that subject matter. No part of a teaching model is more important than setting the stage properly, for if even a few students are not on board before the teacher goes to the next phase—providing information—those few are lost later when they attempt to put together the what (information) with the why (relevance). Unless one knows why, the what is not applicable. It is just an isolated piece of information that stays unused in a student's brain until it eventually is extinguished from lack of use. Thus, one sees why the first step in a lesson (understanding why the information is to be learned) is vital to every student.

This example emphasizes the relationship of why and what. I always did well in mathematics, from algebra through trigonometry; however, plane geometry during the sophomore year bored me. The teacher taught us how to work theorems, but he never explained why we learned them for later use.

A little more than twenty years ago, our son was building a deck for us on the back of our home. I chanced to look out one day and saw him calculating, so I asked what he was doing. He replied, "I'm using the Pythagorean Theorem, Dad."

Never had I observed anyone using the famous theorem, so I asked, "Why?"

Daniel responded, "Do you remember it?"

I said, "Yes. A squared plus B squared equals C squared. So what?"

Daniel smiled and inquired, "What kind of a triangle are A, B, and C part of?"

Showing off my "great" memory, I also smiled and said, "A right triangle, but as I said, so what?"

He chuckled and said, "Come on, Dad, you're a teacher, so how would I be using a right triangle in my work on the deck?"

The light finally dawned as I realized our son had me, so I said, "Oh, oh. You're using the Pythagorean Theorem to square the deck, aren't you?"

About five years ago, I was doing an inservice with teachers at Metro Tech High School in the Kansas City (Missouri) Schools and told that story. During the break, several of the tech teachers came up and explained to me that our ancestors laid out land in Missouri by starting over in the southeast part of the state using the Pythagorean Theorem and continued using it as they plotted the state's land for farming and community purposes.

A successful teacher explains *why* every time new material enters the scene in class, and the successful pedagogue uses enough examples of *why* that the *what* to follow stays in students' memory banks much longer than it would have without lucid examples. That's one important way a teacher is successful, and such teaching enhances the chances for a teacher to increase students' economic well-being as well as the last part of the mission, which follows shortly.

It is obvious that the cliché "Every student can learn" is a useless cliché. The more accurate assertion is, "Every student learns when that student experiences successful teachers."

The third part of the mission, (improve) the quality of life, is one a successful teacher also considers carefully before deciding which subject matter to include because (keep in mind that the students, parents, and principal know the teacher's mission) the teacher wants those aware of her mission to challenge her if they believe the teacher slips up. Overemphasis of this point is almost impossible for reasons revealed in later chapters. It is enough to say here that teamwork is a key concept in STAR Theory, and teamwork implies cooperation between and among the students, parents, teacher, and principal.

Before going to the final part of the teaching mission, an example for improving the quality of life seems necessary, for improving the quality of a student's life is probably the most important facet of the entire mission. Consider the advisability of requiring all students to memorize the U.S. capitals. Does this improve one's economic well-being or quality of life? Hardly. However, requiring students to know where states, provinces, and countries are in relation to one another and to where the student is, surely increases the quality of one's life. Why? This is a question a successful teacher asks her students before teaching them the provinces, states, and countries of North and South America, for instance. Please note the word *asks*. She does not *tell* them unless she wants to eliminate an important part of the lesson, *student pondering*. In fact, the successful teacher asks students *why* often, and they ask her *why* when they question what she is teaching if they do not see the relevance.

The last part of the mission—of all my students—is more than "blowing smoke." If only selected students are part of a teacher's mission, and she works closely only with those who originally come to her wanting to learn, the game of successful schooling is over before it begins. Some might dislike the use of *game* in reference to schooling or teaching, but no word is more accurate. Shakespeare wrote a famous line for Hamlet: "The play's the thing wherein I'll catch the conscience of the King." Then Hamlet staged a play within a play that revealed King Claudius as the murderer of Hamlet's father. Hamlet was playing for keeps, so he used a play to catch the villain.

In schooling and in teaching, the game is for keeps, too. The difference in the game of schooling or teaching, however, is that in STAR Theory, school officials and teachers settle only for students winning while there and when they exit. It has always amazed me that any school or any teacher might be content with less than that. In STAR Theory, when a student submits work that is less than competent, the teacher returns it with suggestions for the student to revise the work to make it competent or quality, preferably the latter. That's real teaching, not posturing. STAR Theory is a game for winners only, and all who play know this from the first pitch to the last, with many hits, runs, and correctable errors in between. Everyone is a winner playing on a winning team.

What are the essential starting points, then, for soundness in pedagogy? (1) A vision or aim with hope, adventure, knowledge, skills, and values to overcome strong denying forces, and with growth in wholesome ways and (2) a teaching mission succinct enough to place front and center in the mind's eye, to communicate how one teaches winners, and to share with each stakeholder. Chapter 3 continues with the necessary strategies used by such pedagogues, and with the qualities those pedagogues need to make the strategies work for all youngsters.

Most success formulas employ three kinds of evidence to validate what their originators assert. The first is used seldom in this book, and that is personal experience. It is used less often because I want you to substitute your own experiences, not mine, as you read, so you'll know these ideas are practical and achievable, as well as good for students. The second is evidence from authorities—that is, from experts in the field. I classify myself as an authority in the field because I have published many articles on educational issues and have labored long and I trust, fruitfully, in the educational vineyards. The third and final kind of evidence is documentation, that is, research results reported from the field. In social science evidence—and teaching is a social science discipline—documentation for many theories abounds. There is also an abundance of authority testimonies, and personal experiences used to validate theories. However, a theory is really a hunch that someone has after looking at all three kinds of evidence.

My hunch has been in the oven for more than a few moons in a professional educational career that began in 1951, preceded by growing up in the home of a hall of fame educator who never uttered a disparaging word to his children (neither did their mother), or to any of his students. My father once said to me at the evening meal where the family always discussed the day's events, "What did you learn in school today, Danny?"

New to the large junior-senior high school after spending my grade school days in small, cordial surroundings with teachers who cared about me, I replied, "I want to tell you about the teacher who's picking on me in this gigantic junior-senior high school, Dad."

"Danny," Dad responded quietly but firmly, "I want you to remember the rest of your school days what I am about to say. Do I have your attention?"

I nodded, and he continued.

"Danny, if everything were just and fair, there would be no need for courage. So, when you believe a teacher is picking on you, tuck that flat tummy of yours in and smile. Do you understand what I have just said?"

Again, I nodded. "Yes, I do, Dad."

Dad's statement that fall evening turned out to be one of the two wisest pieces of advice I've ever received. The other came from Mother when I was several years younger:

Our neighbor next door (I'll call her Mrs. Brown) was Mother's closest friend and a surrogate grandmother to my brother and me. She was in the kitchen talking with Mother, and I happened to be playing outside the open window. Mrs. Brown confided to Mother a serious problem concerning her son. After Mrs. Brown went home, Mother realized I had heard everything, so she called me in and said, "If Mrs. Brown had left her purse here today, would we give it to anyone else?"

"No way!" I answered.

Mother continued, "Mrs. Brown left something here today more valuable than her purse. She left a story that could make many people unhappy. That story is not ours to give to anyone; it is still hers, even though she left it here. So we shall not give it to anyone. Do you understand?"

I did, and I have understood to this day that a confidence or a bit of gossip that a friend has left with me is my friend's, not mine to give to anyone.

I offer these two stories to reinforce the statement about evidence and as a way to help the reader understand who the author of this book is and where he comes from. The book has a few stories (authoritative evidence from me) sprinkled throughout that support STAR Theory. I am a strong proponent of the value of Pygmalion Theory, great literature, reading aloud beginning in utero through one's last days on the planet, dialogues, and storytelling in teaching, and in living with others.

CONCLUSION

The discussion about sound pedagogy continues in the next chapter. Keep in mind that we have penetrated the surface, but have yet to plumb the depths. When we finish plumbing pedagogical depths, we explore the requirements for meeting the thesis assumptions or conditions. To keep it fresh in your mind, it seems important to repeat the thesis from time to time as a successful teacher does in the classroom when what is to come in the lesson depends on students understanding a vital point connected to what's coming. So, here it is again, my friends:

> Sound in pedagogy, the successful teacher creates and maintains a caring relationship with all students, rejects their acts and expressions of irresponsibility, and teaches them responsibility. Ultimately, almost all, if not all, the successful teacher's charges exit competent or better in relevant subject matter and responsible in citizenship.

NOTES

1. Excerpts from the Elbert Hubbard story *A Message to Garcia,* are in a later chapter.

CHAPTER 3

Where Am I Going?

Armed with a vision on a teaching voyage, and with a concise teaching mission fixed front and center in preparing for students, a teacher's next step in the journey to pedagogical soundness is charting where to go in each area she teaches. Some years ago, I read a poem describing the titles of this and the next two chapters. I do not recall where I read this ditty or who wrote it, but it had no title, so I've given it one. With apologies to the unknown author for changes I might have made unintentionally from a distant memory, here is the poem's essence:

> *Three Keys to Stardom*
> There once was a teacher
> Whose principal feature
> Was hidden in quite an odd way.
> Students by millions, possibly zillions,
> Surrounded her all of the day.
> When finally seen by principal and sup
> And asked how she managed the deed,
> She lifted three fingers and said,
> "Any hip teach need only to follow my lead.
> To rise from a zero to big school hero,
> To answer these questions, you'll strive:
> Where am I going?
> How shall I get there?
> And, how will I know I've arrived?"

Simple? No way! The first part of my answer to how she managed the deed—Where am I going?—is one of a teacher's most important decisions: *What do I teach?* Examples: Few argue the importance of teaching the times tables during the middle years of elementary school. Ditto to addition and subtraction, with short and long division later.

Teaching youngsters to print before writing in cursive has also made sense for a long time. Instructing the young in reading completes the elementary part of readin', writin', and 'rithmetic. But, when do we teach them to speak well? In support of doing this, Glasser (1993) proclaimed that helping the young learn to speak convincingly and grammatically is the skill with the highest payoff in the real world. Yet, *when* do we teach them to speak convincingly and grammatically? Is it one of the school curriculum's weak links? Many more of our youth know how to read, write, and figure better than they can convince listeners orally, clearly, and correctly. Doubt it? Listen to people younger than twenty converse and count the crutches—"you know," "uh," "and"—in their conversations. Listen to interviews of athletes by the media, and you will soon agree that fluency and articulateness are usually lacking. Suggestion: No American student should earn a high school diploma without demonstrating at least basic competency in speaking as well as in reading, writing, and figuring. Arguable? Hardly!

In other areas of curriculum, certainly our young need to know how many U.S. senators each state has, the three branches of the federal government, our current president and vice president, the legal voting age, and the countries bordering ours. Youngsters also need to know the general direction one heads from New Orleans to Chicago, or from any major city to another, and know on which continent China and other major countries are located. Geometry students need to understand why they learn the Pythagorean Theorem among others. And it is important for all teachers to stress *why* before and after teaching whatever they believe is worth teaching. The list of essentials goes on and on, of course.

Now comes the biggie: The main interrogative when deciding what to include in and exclude from a required curriculum is this: *At some point in life, does it help us understand and deal with the world we live in more effectively than if we had not learned it?* The *it* in the question refers to what we are considering for curriculum inclusion. Substitute *memorizing state and country capitals* for the *it*, for instance, and answer the question (negatively, I trust). Or, for older students taking chemistry, substitute *memorizing the Periodic Table of Elements* for the *it*. As a determining device, continue substituting everything one teaches to reach a decision on what to include and exclude in measuring student competence in the essentials of a subject that prepares for life. However, the same question can be used for decision making in such subjects as languages of other countries, physics, algebra, chemistry, and others that prepare those youngsters for college and perhaps for something else after college. Similarly, the question is valid for the subject matter in courses like art, music, drama, business, physical education, industrial technology, and others they enroll in to enhance living in the present and as adults, perhaps. Here are a couple of substitutions for the *it* in these areas: *knowing how to create a decent water color picture,* or *gaining skill and knowing which tools to use in creating various wood or metal projects.*

Marilyn vos Savant, listed in the *Guinness Book of World Records* Hall of Fame for highest IQ, answers questions weekly in *Parade* magazine, a part of many Sunday newspapers. She verified the importance of the biggie question in the last paragraph by responding to a reader's question: "It's common to hear students complain that the work they're doing will never come into use in their future lives. What is your opinion?"

That question and vos Savant's response are worthy of inclusion in every teacher preparation institution's requirements for graduates and also is worthy as the lead for every syllabus in our nation's schools. Her response follows:

> That's true much of the time, but that's not why they're doing it. They are laying a foundation of understanding the world, so they can successfully accomplish the work they choose later and not be fools about how it (or they) fit into the overall scheme of things. If they are so narrow that they only know about what they do each day, they'll be both bored and boring. (vos Savant 1994)

Wow! If that does not capture the essence of curriculum choice, what does?

Even the creators of the prestigious SAT and ACT need to consider the question posed that provides a framework for including and excluding curriculum subject matter. Here it is one more time: *At some point in life, does it help us understand and deal with the world we live in more effectively than if we had not learned it?* Keep in mind that the word *effectively* carries a broad meaning. For instance, provided they are taught well, youngsters who learn to sing, draw, paint, or act (and react) in music, art, or drama classes, surely deal with the world more effectively than if they had not learned these skills. If they do not pursue one of these areas in making a living, they still possess skills and *experiences that make their existence more sane, more enjoyable. Thus, they are able to deal with the world they live in more effectively. However, educators still need to scrutinize the various parts of each course to pass the above-mentioned litmus test.*

Consider the possibility of including the biggie question at the beginning of each course syllabus and chalking it in permanently at the top of the main board in each classroom students enter from the time they reach the age of reason, about eight, nine, or ten, depending on individual cerebral development. Add to that the possibility of including immediately under the question, the twenty words or so in the mission of the teacher who occupies the room and who wrote the course syllabus. Now, so that these statements are not ho-hum after a few days, how about opening each class or subject with a reminder of the question and the teaching mission. Consumes no more than a minute or two. Result? When the teacher opens the lesson with an anticipatory set, or as I say, by setting the stage properly, my bet is that the teacher makes certain every student is on board (i.e., understands why the about-to-be-learned subject matter is relevant and worth learning). Let's illustrate this by setting the stage for a lesson on what I am doing at this moment, writing. I use the chalkboard's statement of the question, remind the students of my teaching mission: *Listen to, take seriously, affirm as significant, improve the economic well-being and quality of life of all my students,* then I begin the lesson:

"If you do not believe what I am about to teach is worthy of consuming your time in learning it, or if I am derelict in realizing my teaching mission during the explanation and the dialogues between you and me, please say so. Here goes.

"We have already discussed and agreed on the value to everyone in learning to write well. Today, we discuss and demonstrate the first element in *how* to write well. Yesterday, I quoted our sixteenth president's statement about the importance of the written word. When I was your age, my Dad told me often, 'All that is good is worth repeating,' so here is the gist of Lincoln's words again: One of human beings' two most important inventions is the written symbol. The rail-splitter, by the way, with less than a year of formal schooling, became not only one of our nation's great leaders, but one of its outstanding speakers and writers. When speaking, he was famous for practicing the three Ss: Stand up, Speak up, and Shut up! In writing, he was just as noted for the three Bs: B Brief, B Bright, and B Gone! And the first element of good writing, *content,* was Lincoln's trademark, the chief reason he is so often quoted. To launch today's lesson without an example of his writing is unthinkable. Everyone in the room and in virtually every middle and high school classroom in the United States has read the Gettysburg Address, which he is (falsely) rumored to have written while riding the train to that Pennsylvania town. Few, however, have heard or read Lincoln's second inaugural address. It, too, required fewer than three minutes to deliver in 1865, but surely Lincoln spent much longer composing the literary masterpiece. Listen to the last sentence. Its *content* is the best I can use to point out the purpose of the lesson coming up:

> With malice toward none; with charity for all; with firmness in the right, as God gives us to see the right, let us strive on to finish the work we are in; to bind up the nation's wounds; to care for him who shall have borne the battle, and for his widow and his orphan—to do all that may achieve and cherish a just and lasting peace, among ourselves, and with all nations.

"With that great closing to Lincoln's second inaugural address as inspiration, I am going to teach you why the first element of good writing, *content,* is the most important of the six Cs of good writing, that is, good use of the written symbol. The other five Cs in order of importance are clarity, conciseness, creativity, cogency, and correctness. All are important, but content ranks number 1. Why?"

At this point, I listen to the student offerings and discuss them before going to my prepared lesson. Most of the time, their ideas take care of things; in that case, I simply skip the prepared remarks and review theirs. If this does not happen, here's what I say:

"First, content is the most important C of good writing, because often, if the writer has something new and worth the reader's time and effort to read, the reader is more likely to read it. If not, the remainder of the Cs might not help a great deal. Thus, consider writing about something that interests you. If it does, then how you attend to the remaining Cs can make all the difference in keeping the reader engaged to the end. Content, however, is information for the readers to digest, so gather enough information you believe is new to your readers to avoid putting them to sleep from having heard it all before.

"Second, content does not have to be new to the reader to maintain interest. Often, a reader has seen the material before, but the writer is presenting it this time in a way different enough to entice the reader to continue. We shall discuss this when we arrive at the fourth and fifth most important Cs, *creativity* and *cogency*. However, the content does have to be worthy of reading, so consider the readers' interests, if possible. In school, for instance, students almost always write for an audience of two—the writer and the teacher (it is hoped for parents, also, which makes it an audience of three or four). Keep in mind that the teacher reads many papers, so if you find a topic informative to the teacher, you have made a good start. Any questions?"

"DK, I just never have wanted to write stuff, regardless of the content. It bores me."

"What do you like to do when you don't have to do anything, Jeremy?"

"I like to work on my car; that's my favorite thing in the whole world. I'm goin' to race at the drag strip when I get it fixed up."

"Great! Do yourself and me a big favor, Jeremy. Tell me on paper, step by step, what you have to do to get your car ready to drag. Start the first paragraph with something like, 'Here's what I have remaining to get my car in shape for competition at the drag strip.' In the next few sentences, simply list what these things are. For instance, write, 'The first thing I have to do is overhaul the carburetor. When I finish that in a couple of days, I'll put in new plugs.' You might have other stuff to finish, Jeremy, and probably do, but that's just an example of what you might write. Then, after you list these things in the opening paragraph, explain in a separate paragraph for each thing listed just what is required to complete the operation. In the final paragraph, you might want to predict where you'll finish in the race, based on your specific plan (what you have written) and on the quality of work you've completed when you get everything done. You'll not only have a written blueprint for what you have to do, which is a reminder as you're going along, but you'll write something that'll really interest me because I know little about automobiles. Truly, I don't think such a project will bore you, but if it does, tell me. As you write, you'll find how putting things on paper makes you more exact when you start to complete each operation. I believe you'll also discover that just as the contents of a carburetor are important to successful operation of your car, the content of a paper is pivotal in enticing your readers to read what you have scribed.

"Remember when I asked you a while ago what you liked to do when you didn't have anything else to do? Your answer was an excited,

'Work on my car!' That's what I mean by *content.* Are you game to try, Jeremy?"

With no more abstainers, I've set the stage, and students are on board for my teaching what is meant by *content,* the information of the lesson.

This is a sampling of a dialogue I had with a student some years back as I was demonstrating for teachers how to teach an important lesson. I was the principal in that school, so I had developed caring relationships with myriad students, and the ones I had not yet related to personally knew me through their friends or through the school's daily announcements.

Thus, when setting the stage for teaching the first of the six Cs of good writing or anything else, be certain to include the students and their reactions. There is no better way to get everyone on board for learning than including as many youngsters, especially the feet-draggers, as possible.

This is an excellent time to reinforce the subject matter of chapter 1, ". . . develops and maintains a caring relationship with all students." Had I not developed such a relationship with Jeremy, the feet-dragger (or friends of Jeremy who knew me or specific things about me), and developed writing's importance and interest, Jeremy's receptivity to my question and resulting suggestions could have been zilch! Instead, he spent tons of time on the essay about fixing his hot rod. His paper was a little shy of quality, but it was amazingly competent.

By the way, this is part of Where Am I Going? not How Shall I Get There? because teachers cannot be certain that what they are teaching is where they want to go with the youngsters until they attempt to set the stage properly and bring everyone on board. Occasionally you'll see that students point out flaws in choosing some subject matter.

CONCLUSION

Recapping, the first need is a teacher vision of expectations during a teaching voyage (career); next is a concise teaching mission front and center when involved on that voyage; third, the following pivotal Where Am I Going? question is in mind, in the course syllabus, and on the classroom chalkboard: *At some point in life, does it help us understand and deal with the world we live in more effectively than if we had not learned it?*

Even in districts that supply syllabi with detailed answers to Where Am I Going? in every area of curriculum, the biggie question needs to be asked about the inclusions in those syllabi. The biggie question's answers ensure periodic scrutiny. Remember, even quality can be improved.

A teacher is now on the road to pedagogical success and is ready to work with the subject of chapter 4, How Shall I Get There? Of the chapters on pedagogy in this book, this one contains material that requires years to master; however, fret not. Instead, follow the enthusiasm of Tennyson's Ulysses in his famous poem of the same name:

> Come my friends,
> 'Tis not too late to seek a newer world.
> Push off, and sitting well in order smite
> The sounding furrows; for my purpose holds
> To sail beyond the sunset, and the baths
> Of all the western stars, until I die.
> It may be that the gulfs will wash us down:
> It may be we shall touch the Happy Isles,
> And see the great Achilles, whom we knew.
> Tho' much is taken, much abides; and tho'
> We are not now that strength which in old days
> Moved earth and heaven; that which we are, we are;
> One equal temper of heroic hearts,
> Made weak by time and fate, but strong in will
> To strive, to seek, to find, and not to yield.

On the voyage to teaching greatness, one meets many living Achilles, and touches uncountable happy isles while sailing beyond the sunset and the baths of all the western stars. But the gulfs shall wash none of us down if, as Cavafy wrote in *Ithaca,* our thoughts remain lofty, and if select emotions imbue our spirits and our bodies.

CHAPTER 4

How Shall I Get There?

Implementing the preceding chapters' recommendations is an essential part of peopling our schools with successful teachers and thus, with a plethora of competent and responsible students. This chapter, however, contains material fundamental to and at the heart of that goal. The next few paragraphs hint strongly at this assertion, and the Simon and Bloom studies that follow are the cleanup hitters in the chapter's early innings. However, when Simon and Bloom clear the bases, no one is out, and the rally has just begun. "How to teach well" is a skill devoutly to be wished and long in the making, but master pedagogues are a joy to behold.

According to the tenets that follow, some readers might recognize themselves as experts, masters, or teaching gurus. Please continue reading to verify. I probably reached mastery some time in my forties, many more than a few years into my career, but amazingly (not really), I continue to learn things every day that hone my teaching skills. As an enthusiastic, excited neophyte back in 1951, I didn't realize I was a member of the know-little party. It is just as exciting and refreshing today to walk into a classroom or a great hall, speak one-to-one with a student, or spend a few hours at the computer keyboard writing what I have learned.

Now, to the chase! In our modern era, sometimes teachers report for a new position, and awaiting them are syllabi detailing what to teach—*Where Am I Going?* The syllabi might also house specifics about how to measure whether the concerned teachers' students have learned what they were scheduled to have learned—*How Will I Know I've Arrived?* Once in a while, these syllabi provide hints on how to teach—*How Shall I Get There?* Two of the parts often work at least fairly well; that is, they attempt to provide consistency among district teachers in what to teach and in measuring at least some of what they have taught. However, only an unthinking robot fails to *expand* on printed directions outlining how to teach. It is hardly possible not to embellish on the how-to-teach suggestions because *teaching style* (how to teach) separates human beings from computers, from books, and from all else inanimate.

Do not misunderstand. Teacher preparation institutions employ many outstanding pedagogues who save undergrads and grads hours of treading water by offering intelligent suggestions about how to teach. The same applies to mentors at the school and district levels who take neophytes under their wings, apprise them of shortcuts, and expand their minds with ideas on the subject of teaching. Even lucid authors like the late Madeline Hunter, Rudolph Dreikurs, John Dewey, or the contemporary gurus William Glasser, Deborah Meier, and many others assist willing teachers through the written page. And syllabi are useful in offering common-sense ideas that many use. In the end, though, diligence and time are necessary to develop this area—How Shall I Get There?—before mastery salutes striving pedagogues.

Some individuals, however, never become consummate teachers because they simply do not have it! The *it* in this case might be personality, patience, unconditional positive regard for all students, genuineness, high empathy, disposition, perseverance, or other human traits necessary to achieve mastery (success)—that is, to become experts in the art and science of teaching. Additionally, some fail because they do not connect with the proper gurus, others because they are not diligent. Teaching, after all, is a social science, and social scientists work primarily with people's minds and emotions, which vary greatly. Our teacher preparation institutions and school leaders must stress the importance and the nobility of teachers as social scientists who work with minds and emotions. They need to use many case-study scenarios and clinical experiences after thoroughly grounding aspiring masters in the principles of sociology and psychology. Neophytes can then more readily understand what awaits them in the schoolhouse trenches. This leads to supportive research that illustrates and reinforces the absolute necessity of two factors mentioned earlier—diligence (directed properly) and time.

Nobel prize-winning economist Herbert Simon, also a pioneering investigator in computer simulation of intelligence, found that experts are people in a field who understand and can process the "patterns of symbols" in that area of life (Griessman, 1987). Grand master chess players, for example, are experts who have stored in their brains a large number of patterns they recognize when the patterns occur on boards in front of them.

Experts are individuals who recognize and deal with more patterns than nonexperts. Often they see patterns they cannot explain, an ability called *intuition*. Simon found that most experts have tens of thousands of such patterns or chunks of knowledge stored in their brains, and it takes a minimum of ten years to develop this level of mastery. Even child prodigies like world chess champion Bobby Fisher and the inimitable Wolfgang Amadeus Mozart are examples. Neither achieved mastery in fewer than ten years.

In addition to Simon's findings, University of Chicago researcher Benjamin Bloom studied the careers of world-class concert pianists, sculptors, research mathematicians, neurologists, Olympic swimmers, and tennis champions. He found the average time between the pianists' first lessons and the time they won international competitions was just over seventeen years (Griessman, 1987). Research mathematicians and neurologists, he found, required even longer to hit their professional strides.

Of course, future masters (experts) do not spend the intervening time passively waiting for expertise to develop by itself. Three requirements are necessary to reach mastery: continued education, disciplined practice, and support from others (Griessman 1987).

Citing this study as the keynote speaker in sixty conferences for beginning teachers sponsored by the Missouri Elementary and Secondary School Principals Associations, I reached more than eight thousand new teachers in October and November during a seven-year period. Naturally, many were on the edges of their seats listening for any suggestions I had to help them "survive" year number 1 as a pedagogue. After citing from Griessman's book, I followed immediately with, "And so, please continue to have hope." Then, I shared with these folks what follows. Remember, we lose half of them within five years after they begin teaching because we do not provide, at least the ones with potential, the support to succeed.

I told them that teaching probably requires more than ten years for most to become successful, experts, masters, gurus. Looking back on fifty years as an educator who has observed more than two thousand teachers in classroom pursuits, I strongly believe the average time required these days to reach mastery in teaching (for those who pay the price) is twelve to fifteen years; however, many assumptions underlie this belief, and they follow:

1. Continue your education. Start on the master's degree immediately after your first year of teaching. Before that, you have no frames of reference to put the information gleaned from master's degree courses. Find a qualified mentor (adviser in the graduate school) and stay in touch during pursuit of the degree. Write each other e-mails; telephone one another; arrange lunch; establish a caring relationship. If the graduate adviser is not adequately helping early on during your teaching voyage, change. Good mentors are in position to help graduate students realize their aims for many years, and they are master teachers themselves. Choose carefully and find another if you outgrow the one you have chosen. I cannot overestimate the importance of this point! Interning physicians have mentors, and our work with the minds and emotions of the young is as important as theirs.

My first mentor was Don Davis at Emporia (Kansas) State Teachers College. We stayed in touch many years as he moved to a university in Detroit and finally, to the presidency of a small college in Arkansas. When Dr. Don asked me to join him on that voyage as his dean of instruction, I had just completed the doctorate and was in the first year of a high school principalship in a northern suburb of Kansas City. Yearning to continue learning from that sage, but with a young family, I believed I could not afford to leave the significantly higher paying position in Kansas City. In light of the fourth assumption in this book, I might have made the wrong decision, but I was not as wise then. Most educators have similar, large decisions on their journeys, so remember to learn and continue learning from the sages (*Ithaca*). This has been one of the most effective ways of learning for hundreds of years. Remember the apprentices of yore? If each interning pedagogue apprenticed with a master for a year, the results in youngsters' achievement and citizenship would fly through the roof!

2. Do not stop with a master's degree. Continue to an educational specialist program, even to a doctorate if it profits your vision, and if you possess that kind of motivation and learning style. If financially able, pursue graduate degrees from different institutions in various parts of the country. Strive to become a true citizen of the world. Not only shall you become a more effective pedagogue, you shall somewhat sooner and more likely understand ". . . the meaning of an Ithaca."

3. Seventeenth-century English writer and scientist, Francis Bacon, wrote that reading makes the full person, conversation the ready person, and writing the exact person. Graduate school is not the only kind

of continuing education that enhances pedagogical soundness. For instance, set a goal to read several classics a year and take copious notes on what you've learned from each. Keep these notes in a handy place like your school desk and study them from time to time when you have spare moments. As a septuagenarian, I still do. One is from an essay by W. Somerset Maugham in which he wrote something like this: Can you read in a way that makes you think and finally produce something with the look and taste of your own mind upon it? Ever since I read that challenge, probably fifty years ago, I've been jotting down ideas of my own from things I've read that have piqued my curiosity. I'd never have done this had I not read Maugham's *The Razor's Edge* when I was a teenager in the South Pacific during World War II. After reading that wonderful book, I focused on doing what Maugham's protagonist did. Larry searched for the meaning of life, and so did I after returning from the war. And my search has yielded findings similar to Joshua's response to the question, "What is life about?" in one of the many esoteric, intriguing, simple, and lucidly written Joseph Girzone books. If interested, you'll find Joshua's response to the question on page 127 in the hardback edition of *Joshua, the Homecoming* (1999). It is beautiful.

Joining professional organizations and reading their literature is also requisite in becoming a master. Truly professional English teachers, for instance, join the National Council of Teachers of English and read interesting-looking articles from the monthly *English Journal*. Whatever the subject matter or the teaching level (as in elementary school teaching) background, join the related organizations and read. Regular reading of the *Kappan,* especially the research section, puts many a leg up on reaching mastery sooner. Keep up with what is going on in school research. Also, read the local newspaper to stay abreast of happenings in the community and the world. Continue to fill yourself your whole life by reading good literature.

If you try a new idea in the classroom and the idea works, exercise your writing skills by submitting the results to the local paper or a professional journal. It is important to begin publishing early in one's career. Set an aim to write and to publish at least one article a year at first. Later, increase that to two or more. Eventually, perhaps a monograph or a full-length book is in you. To assist, purchase Strunk and White's *The Elements of Style* and keep it in your reading room. Every teacher needs the "little book," as Strunk referred to it. Read, mark, re-

read, mark, and continue re-reading and marking until it and your own writing make you more exact.

I'll respond now rather than later: "You are welcome!"

Following Bacon's advice for readying oneself, find fellow teachers or friends in other fields who like to discuss ideas, not people, and set regular discussion sessions. As a start, you might all want to read the same book or article and discuss how it can help you grow in your various professions or as human beings. You may also wish to do this with the classics or with popular, but not pulp, books. Call all-American teacher Vicki Barmann at Winnetonka High School in the North Kansas City (Missouri) Schools (816–413–5500) if you'd like advice on how to start such a group. Continue to read, confer, and write to realize your potential even long after you complete the degrees you've sought.

4. Set another aim after the first week or two of each school year: Call two students' parents each evening there is school the next day. First, discuss each youngster's strengths (every young person has these) then ask each parent to tell you the youngster's strengths as a family member. Let the conversation turn as it will from there, and close by inviting the parent to call or come see you any time a need arises. You'll be amazed how much better you'll know each student by communicating with a parent. And, if you are a young teacher, the parents are probably older and wiser and can contribute to your growth—if you listen closely. A fringe benefit is the passage of school bonds and levies as a result of this simple idea. If every teacher called parents of two students each of those nights during the school year, consider the good will and respect the calling teachers have generated. Above all, keep the conversations positive.

5. Purchase a videotape and use it to capture strong minilessons (no longer than fifteen to twenty minutes) for your study and edification. Tape as many different teaching-learning strategies as possible. If you are proud of one, ask your principal or a fellow teacher to view it with you while you provide commentary. At the conclusion, ask for ideas to help you grow. When you run out of tape, buy another and another. You'll astound yourself years later as you review them from year one to the present in observing your voyage to mastery. Who handles the camera? One of your students if old enough. If not, borrow a youngster old enough from a teacher friend in the same school for these sessions. Athletic coaches have used this method for years to foster their own and the student-athletes' growth. Why not classroom teachers?

6. Attend professional conferences when they have marquis participants on the program. If you cannot attend, purchase and study audio
or videotapes of them. When attending, converse with many you deem
can help you grow. Attend with prepared questions like, "Do you have
suggestions for teaching higher-level thinking skills successfully?"
"Can you pass along an idea that has worked in getting anti-school
parents turned around?" "Any hints on testing youngsters at the higher
levels of thinking?"

Listen to audiotapes on extended automobile trips of thirty minutes
or more. If the tape is not finished when you complete the journey,
finish it as soon as you can so you are able to take notes on good ideas.
Many physicians do this from home or the office to visit their patients
in the hospitals and then back to wherever they go next. Audiobook
classics also help us grow.

7. You are a teacher; thus, you are a speaker. Join a local Toastmasters Club chapter and improve your oral skills. I belonged for several
years and as our local club's representative, reached the Toastmasters
International Speech Contest finals in Minneapolis when I was in my
thirties. No speech course has ever prepared me for speaking or conversing with others like Toastmasters. Why? Because it is learning by
doing as well as learning by listening and reading. I recommend it to
every teacher, principal, superintendent, and parent. It's as good as, if
not better than, a Dale Carnegie course. I realize teachers are not supposed to talk much, but rather encourage their students to talk and to
do, but we all talk more than we read or write, so why not do it convincingly and grammatically!

8. In addition to your graduate school mentors, find one in the
school/district where you teach and pick the mentor's brain, visit her
classes (ask your principal to pinch-hit in your class while you
observe), dine, take breaks, and go to meetings with your local guru
(mentor). More about this in chapter 6, but keep in mind that apprentic-
ing to masters is a long-verified way to reach quality.

9. Leave the television off in the evening once in a while and consider doing one or more of the following: Spend the time reading a
good book; write an article; invite friends over for stimulating conversation, or dine with them in a nice restaurant; listen to some great music
while conversing with family members; find a good fine arts movie
theater and view a four-star film, or rent one; attend a high-brow music
concert; take a long walk in the woods (if it's safe), or in an up-scale
neighborhood; visit some of your students' parents; attend a school and

a district function; sit back and ponder awhile; enjoy your best girl or guy friend on a Coke or malt date (spouses qualify here, too); and the list is just beginning. After all, this life is not a practice run; it's the real thing!

Although I offered the preceding ideas to beginning teachers, many apply to all of us, no matter how many years we've labored in the teaching vineyards. Most of the ideas have to do with continued education of one kind or another, but disciplined practice and support from others were in there, also. For instance, viewing and re-viewing videotaped minilessons you've done leads to disciplined practice, and spending time with family and friends is a way to stay sane.

The next step in how to teach well is to study student learning styles. I have been a fan of Rita and Ken Dunn for many years, but there are others. Ask your guru for a recommendation and become an expert on this subject. Did you know, for instance, that the five most powerful elements of learning style are (1) light, (2) sound, (3) perseverance, (4) intake, and (5) design? Only one is inherent—perseverance. Analytics like lots of light, no bothersome sounds, no eating or drinking, traditional chairs when they study. They also persevere until they finish tasks. Globals, on the other hand, would rather study without much light, but they want music or some kind of naked sound to keep them on task, and they want food and drink and soft chairs or pillows on the floor while they study. Still, they find it tough to stick with it. It's no wonder that in U.S. schools with skads of analytics as teachers, analytics get the perks, but the globals are considered the jerks! Sad but true. Of course, many, many more elements of learning style exist, so do not neglect this important aspect of how to teach the young. Beginning to see why diligence and time are required in reaching mastery (success)?

Although we know much about how people learn, we do not possess all the insights into learning. But we have advanced significantly and can apply many of the theories and principles with confidence that we can predict results beyond chance alone. In other words, although we are social scientists who deal mainly with people's minds and emotions, we have gathered enough data through the years to understand how most people learn. The danger is picking and choosing only parts of favorite theories and applying what we *feel* rather than know, is important. Thus, we distort many theories beyond recognition and workability.

This is not a treatise on learning theory, but it is one on a theory that proposes a means to increase significantly the numbers of students exiting our schools successfully; that is, exiting competent or better in relevant subject matter and responsible in citizenship. For that reason, it is necessary to pick a learning theory compatible with STAR Theory. I have verified a theory workable with thousands of youngsters. It is William Glasser's *Choice Theory* (1998). Another Glasser book, mentioned earlier, filled with principles of psychiatry that relate to teaching the young, normal and otherwise, is *Reality Therapy* (1965). Successful teachers do many of the things with their students that reality therapists do with their patients. Successful teachers, for example, take their students forward from where they meet them. So do reality therapists. Neither believes in the old-fashioned idea that something in the student's (patient's) past caused incurable aberrant behavior, and the teacher (therapist) must discover what that was before progress can be made. Successful teachers, like successful reality therapists, develop strong, caring relationships with their people, maintain these relationships, reject irresponsible expressions and acts, then teach responsible ones. What could make more sense?

Getting back to choosing a learning theory, for a lucid explanation of Glasser's Choice Theory, read chapters 4, 5, and 6 of *The Quality School*, keeping in mind that he called it *Control Theory* then. For an even better and more thorough grasp of the principles and practices, read *Choice Theory* (1998).

Compatible with the foregoing is what we have learned about how students are turned on to learning, more formally called student motivation. Nothing is more important for teachers to know and understand en route to success than the fruits of research on the topic. How often, for instance, does one hear that a baby is not interested in walking and talking? Seldom. They learn these vital skills mainly by modeling the behavior of Mother, Dad, and other caretakers. Almost all children continue to relish learning about the world they live in for at least several years, especially if adults around them verbalize regularly and positively with the children. The passion for learning soon wears off for many, however, and by the time they reach adolescence, as many as one in every four drop out of school. Sad, even tragic, for many.

The National Association of Secondary School Principals has kept its members (mostly middle, junior, and senior high principals) abreast of all kinds of educational research for decades, and Linda S. Lumsden (1994) wrote an exceptional article summarizing the research.

Lumsden pointed out it is important for teachers to know the reasons or goals that lie beneath youngsters' involvement or lack thereof in learning activities. Many might be equally motivated to perform a task, but the sources of their motivation may differ. For example, a student who does an activity for its own sake, for the enjoyment it provides, the learning it allows, or the feelings of accomplishment, is intrinsically motivated (Lepper 1988). An extrinsically motivated youngster does it for a reward or to avoid a consequence unconnected from the activity. Examples are grades, stickers, and teacher approval.

Lumsden wrote that, according to Brophy (1987), motivation to learn is a competence acquired through experience but stimulated mostly directly through modeling (familiar word?), communication of expectations, and direct instruction or socialization by significant others like parents and teachers.

Lumsden continued by stating that home environs shape the initial attitudes the young develop toward learning. Educators and parents, attend closely to Lumsden's following assertion from the findings: Nurturing children's natural curiosity about the world by welcoming questions, encouraging exploring, and furnishing resources that enlarge their worlds, parents give their children a message that learning is worthwhile, frequently fun, and satisfying. When children are reared in homes that nurture senses of self-worth, competence, autonomy, and self-efficacy, parents have children more apt to accept risks inherent in learning. That is key in child rearing, so please underline, use in your own rearing of children, and be certain to share it with parents of the youngsters you teach. Please, go back and read it again before reading on.

When children do not view themselves as able, their propensities to take part in risky or challenging pursuits and their capacities to tolerate and cope with failure plummet! Again, do the same with this statement!

Enter the school leaders and the teachers: When children start school, they begin forming beliefs about school-related successes and failures. The sources to which children attribute their successes and failures have important implications for how they approach and cope with learning, Lumsden reported.

Beliefs teachers have about teaching and learning, and the nature of expectations they hold for students also exert a powerful influence (Raffini 1993). Stipek (1988) noted that students expect to learn if their teachers expect them to learn. This squares with Pygmalion Theory discussed earlier, and is the chief trait I have looked for in potential teachers for years. Expecting all their students to learn is resident in all STARs.

Schoolwide goals, policies, and procedures also interact with classroom climate and practices to affirm or alter students' increasingly complex learning-related attitudes and beliefs (Lumsden 1994). And developmental changes constitute one more part of the motivational web. For example, although young children maintain high success expectations even in the face of repeated failure, older students do not. Although younger children tend to see effort as uniformly positive, older children view it as a double-edged sword (Ames 1990). To them, failure following high effort appears to carry more negative consequences—especially for their self-concept of ability—than failure resulting from minimal or no effort. No wonder school leaders are so important in setting an atmosphere in their schools.

Back to intrinsic motivation, are there advantages? A growing body of evidence suggests there are (Lumsden 1994). When intrinsically motivated, students employ strategies that demand more effort, which enable them to process information more deeply (Lepper 1988).

Condry and Chambers (1978) found that when students were confronted with complex intellectual tasks, intrinsically oriented students used more logical information-gathering and decision-making strategies than did those who were extrinsically motivated. The former also preferred moderately challenging tasks; the latter leaned toward low-difficulty tasks. They are inclined to put forth minimal effort to get maximal rewards (Lepper 1994). Lepper, Condry, and Chambers' findings should be required reading for all who enter teaching. Although every task cannot be intrinsic in nature, and perhaps should not be, these findings suggested that when teachers use intrinsically motivating activities, several benefits accrue.

HOW CAN WE FOSTER MOTIVATION TO LEARN IN SCHOOL?

Students' motivational patterns follow them from year to year, but it is essential for each new teacher to see herself capable of stimulating student motivation to learn in her classroom setting regardless of baggage attendant to students entering there (Brophy 1987). Brophy's finding should be part of every school of education's preparation of teachers about to enter the profession. Each school principal needs to follow up when these neophytes come to her school to teach.

Classroom climate is important. If students experience the classroom as a caring, supportive place with a sense of belonging, and everyone there is valued and respected, they participate more fully in learning processes, Lumsden continued. Sounds like STAR Theory, doesn't it! Task size in the classroom also affects motivation to learn. Tasks should be challenging but achievable, and naturally, relevance also promotes motivation, as does placing tasks in proper contexts within the student's frame of reference. When one asks whether tasks are applicable in the real world, the response must be affirmative (Lepper 1994). Short-term goals assist youngsters in associating effort with success (Stipek 1988). Verbally noting specific task purposes as tasks are introduced is also beneficial (Brophy 1986). Earlier, I had mentioned the necessity of getting everyone on board before teaching the material. Brophy has verified this in his research.

Introduce extrinsic rewards with extreme caution, for they have the potential of reducing existing intrinsic motivation. Dangerous waters! Rewarding students for learning often extinguishes any inherent desire to learn for the thrill of learning. Highlight and place the preceding statement on your desk because the temptation to reward the young materially for achievement is great, but it is a testimony to ineffective teaching when it is done too often.

Schoolwide goals either dilute or enhance teachers' classroom efforts. To enhance motivation to learn, school-level policies and actions stress learning, mastery, and effort rather than relative performance and competition (Maehr and Midgley 1991). Please remember that statement, school leaders! A principal's dynamic, supportive leadership is to be devoutly appreciated.

HOW ABOUT UNMOTIVATED YOUNGSTERS?

No matter how untoward the behavior, at the heart is the student's desire to protect the sense of self-worth (Raffini 1993). Modeling, socialization, and practice exercises, called *attribution retraining,* often help discouraged young people see the value of learning. The goals of such training are to concentrate on tasks; retrace steps to find mistakes; or figure alternative ways to approach a problem instead of giving up; and attribute failures to insufficient effort, lack of information, or reliance on ineffective strategies rather than to lack of ability (Brophy 1986).

Other useful ideas to help the unmotivated: Portray effort as an investment rather than a risk; portray skill development as incremental and domain-specific; focus on mastery (Brophy 1986).

Lumsden concluded that the payoff for having students who value learning for its own sake is priceless. It is crucial for parents, teachers, and school leaders to concentrate on engendering, maintaining, and re-sparking students' motivation to learn. The preceding section is worthy of reproducing and placing on your teacher's desk for re-reading from time to time.

CONCLUSION

Writers have produced tomes on how to teach. Later chapters here house more good stuff: chapter 6 includes ideas successful district teachers can use in mentoring others striving for mastery. Chapter 11 offers a system all district teachers utilize in working with recalcitrant students. How to teach—How Shall I Get There?—is basic to the pro-duction of school and districtwide successful teachers. Stating this with more flair, I say, "Stay tuned for more on education's most exhilarating topic—teaching successfully with pizzazz!"

CHAPTER 5

How Will I Know I've Arrived?

One of the most important and intriguing things about schooling is the idea of measurement, or How Will I Know I've Arrived? For the purpose of this book, the assumption is that, to a certain extent, people are able to measure what young people have learned. Let me ask you a question. Please answer to the best of your ability before you continue reading this chapter. Here's the question: What do you remember learning in elementary school that you still use much of the time as an adult?

When I answered this question, here are some things I recalled without pausing. I recalled learning to sharpen the reading skills Mother had taught me during my preschool years. I also learned in school how to print then write cursively, how to add, subtract, multiply, and divide (first short then long division). I learned what fractions were and how to add, subtract, multiply, and divide them. I learned how to do the same with decimals. I remembered learning what a sentence consisted of and how to write one, starting by capitalizing the first letter of the first word. I learned some punctuation, too, but I do not recall how much then and how much later. I also learned parts of speech and how to diagram sentences (that might have been in junior high). I recalled learning how to spell and how to hone my reading skills by using sounds the teacher flashed on cards in front of the class, and by doing well on the spelling test at the end of each week from a list provided at the beginning of the week. I remembered learning how America was discovered and settled. I especially recalled the Pilgrims settling in Massachusetts at Plymouth because we lived in Providence, Rhode Island, at that time and had a play in class about the Pilgrims. I played Miles Standish, although I really wanted to play John Alden so I could have Priscilla (I don't use that stuff today, but it was fun and has helped me know who I am). I remembered learning that the Pilgrims and the

Indians celebrated together the first Thanksgiving with a big feast. I remembered that Jamestown was settled in 1607—even before the Pilgrims came. I remembered that Roger Williams discovered Rhode Island, and Massasoit was one of many famous American Indians. Today, we call these original Americans *Native Americans*. Although I don't use most of what I recalled about our history, it is part of what makes me an American and who I am, and I believe that is as important as anything we learn through our lives, other than reading, writing, figuring, and speaking well.

I could go on but have made the point. Teachers measured (tested) our knowledge and skills on much of the preceding, but we learned lots of things no one measured, including the names of my grade school teachers, but I remember every one of them because they were great teachers, and because we loved each other. The sad thing is that I failed to write each at least one letter and say, "Thank you, Miss Burton, Miss Sheridan, Miss Lewis, Miss Schmall, Miss Sheeder, and Mr. Sollenberger!" These were my first six teachers in the order I had the privilege of knowing them, and without exception, they were superb pedagogues. I can still see in my mind's eye what each looked like in build and in countenance.

The things I learned after grade school are fuzzier, although they are more recent. However, I believe I remember and use a much higher percentage of the things I learned in grade school than in all my other schooling because those things were so basic to everyday living. For instance, I took four years of college-bound mathematics in high school, but about all I've used in my real world is what I learned in grade school arithmetic. I suppose I used some algebra in the two statistics courses I took in graduate school (so I could do a dissertation), but I haven't used much else. If my teachers had taught me why we learned theorems and equations, perhaps I would remember using some of those concepts as an adult. However, I did not know at the time I learned ideas in higher mathematics that I would not use these ideas. Had I done some other things for a living, I might have needed concepts in those math courses. Thus, recall chapter 3 and what Marilyn vos Savant wrote, and it is easy to justify having taken two courses in algebra, one in plane geometry, a semester of solid geometry, and a semester of trigonometry.

The main point in beginning this chapter—How Will I Know I've Arrived?—is that we need to study judiciously what and how to measure and what not to measure. You have just read one of the most important assertions in the business of educating the young, so here it is again in italics: *We need to study judiciously what and how to measure and what not to measure!* Here is why: A more judicious approach to deciding what and how to measure student achievement is the elimination of much information that is unimportant compared with the vast amount of information entering our world at a more rapid rate than ever. Testing (measuring) our young people on how and where to find information, and on higher-order thinking skills is the focus of an intelligent testing program. Certainly, students need to know facts, lots and lots of facts, so they know how and where to find things, and how to proceed up the thought ladder to comprehension, application, analysis, synthesis, and evaluation. But when we eliminate the unimportant lower-level stuff we have been testing them on for decades, we have the time, and more of it, to focus on the valuable.

For example, consider telling the story of world and U.S. history in compelling ways, but not testing on many of the dates or obscure events. I have gone by many classrooms like Dick Dunlap's and Roy Williams's, and I simply had to back up, go in, and sit down because these master storytellers "grabbed" my curiosity. Every school has teachers like them. Surely, I had heard or read this information, or some of it, years ago, but these masters were weaving their magic on the youngsters and on me. However, I have also asked to take the same tests in history classes that students take, and as they sit and take them, also have asked teachers to grade mine with the students' and give me the results. I usually received a low grade. When I sat later to talk with the teacher, I reminded the teacher that I was an "A" student in history in high school and college. In fact, several times in high school when our U.S. history teacher was ill, Principal Detwiler paid me, a high school junior, almost $6 a day to sub as the teacher (during World War II, when subs were scarce).

When the teachers and I discussed the tests, I suggested that instead of attempting to measure student memory on mundane things they forget before they exit the course or high school, why not test them on the big issues and inform them that the rest of the story is free. A few of the big issues may be:

1. In a complete sentence that is clear, concise, and mechanically correct, present one major reason the North and South fought each other in the War Between the States.
2. In no more than two complete sentences that are clear, concise,

and mechanically correct, explain why President Truman did not warn the Japanese that we were going to drop the atom bomb?

3. Although criticized by opponents for causing our nation to spend big money (at the time), Jefferson and Seward, separated by more than half a century of U.S. history, had something in common that helped accent their names in the history books. In no more than three complete, clear, concise, and mechanically correct sentences, explain respectively, the commonality, the specific deed each accomplished, and why each accomplishment is important to the United States today.

4. Although this twentieth-century president is not remembered for great achievements in office, he said something that reflects as much what the United States means as anything. He said, "The business of America is business." Use this president's name in a complete, clear, concise, and mechanically correct sentence that paraphrases his statement's meaning.

All these are worth knowing because the responses help define who we are and some of what was and is important in making us who we are. Additionally, as Marilyn vos Savant wrote, it's important so "you won't be both bored and boring." Also, the requirement of writing complete, clear, concise, and mechanically correct sentences is an excellent exercise in improving our youth's writing skills, skills that contribute to student focus. Focus is often overlooked as a goal in educating our nation's young, and such measurement (testing) as the above suggestions, assists greatly in students' reaching that important destination—the ability to focus. Lincoln was one of the United States's best examples of a person who focused his thoughts through preciseness in his use of words and sentence structure. All pedagogues could do much worse than study the great man's speeches, letters, and writings (not his poetry, which was unexceptional). Abraham Lincoln was one of the country's most gifted and focused writers and speakers.

If history teachers limit the number of questions in each major and minor examination of student achievement, and employ statements similar to the preceding examples, they soon fall into the rhythm of evaluating the answers with alacrity.

History and other social studies courses are not the only ones educators reassess when contemplating how to measure student learning. Every discipline comes under scrutiny in efforts to open more slots of time for teaching the right stuff. One more example serves a purpose.

Since schooling began, teachers have been trying to measure what students have read by requiring book reports. Nothing turns off youngsters more than these. So, how does one measure what youngsters read? Just ask them to tell what they have learned from the book. That not only exercises their higher-order thinking processes, it presents students with an opportunity to make what they've read part of their own lives by relating what the author wrote to their own lives and values. It is important to ask students to relate specifics from the book read in relating what they have learned.

Remember what I wanted to do after reading Maugham's *The Razor's Edge*? I wanted to return from war and discover what life was about, and I eventually did, at least to my satisfaction. Such an exercise in measuring what students have learned from a book requires *focus,* and when students focus, they write and speak more clearly if writing and speaking are required. For instance, try the following: "Relate specific examples from the book and explain what you have learned that has helped or, perhaps, shall help you." When young people read with this in mind, they eventually exit school with sharply focused minds that are able to use what they have read.

After deciding what to include and to leave out of testing, remember to call to mind that the secondary reinforcement in Reinforcement Theory is the pleasure we derive from learning something, and that pleasure is what makes the learning stick. For example, when a child answers the question, "What does two plus two equal?" with "Four," and the teacher responds, "That is correct; well done, Joan," the primary reinforcement is relief that the answer is right, and the secondary reinforcement is the pleasure associated with hearing the good news that her response was the correct one. Such teacher recollection and practice of using meaningful, not menial, testing helps cause positive changes in a school's test scores, student grades, and confidence. And confidence building is a large part of our job, but few stress it enough. Isn't it interesting that research backs us up when we follow a correct student response with hurrahs? Every person wants to be right, and recognition for such correctness is often overlooked by pedagogues.

More than once in a while try a hearty, "Well done, George!" or "Nice work, Smitty!" or "You're really on a roll, Jeannie!" or "Wow! I knew you were smart, but that answer is something I never would have thought of. You've opened new territory. Thank you, Mr. John Cartright!" or "You've explained your answer more capably than you've ever done before. I know this is the beginning of greatness,

Sam!" or "Do you know what, Susie? YOU ARE RIGHT!" or "I applaud your sagacity, Ms. Samantha!" or "Is that your final answer, Annie? I certainly hope so because no one can improve on the one you just gave. Bravo!" As a matter of fact—a research fact, that is—make such primary and secondary reinforcement responses a habit, for no human being tires of hearing nice things about personal performance.

Caution! Make certain when you verbally applaud behavior that it is justified and that the laudatory remarks are about specific behaviors, not about general or fuzzy stuff. We also know that if praise comes for things undeserved or not understood, the praise becomes addictive or not meaningful; and either result can lead to trouble. So, please be sure that specific, deserved secondary reinforcement praise is what you offer, nothing less and nothing more.

Now, let us discuss the kinds of measurement appropriate to determining how you know you've arrived. First, eliminate true-false questions unless you require a simple sentence explanation of why the answer is true or false. This sounds elementary because surely every person preparing to enter the field of teaching has learned in a test-and-measurements course along the way that true-false questions are not effective measuring instruments. Even if youngsters do well on them, teachers do not really know what they have measured. Why do you suppose major testing organizations use only multiple-choice questions in the area of objective tests and not antiquated true-false interrogatives?

Next, cease implementing matching questions. These are the most inefficient of all objective questions. With fifteen or twenty key words or phrases on one side and a like number or more across from them, students might get one or two wrong then see that they have sinned when right answers show up later, and the debacle begins. Matching exercises are glorified multiple-choice questions without the time and thought needed by teacher testers to discover what their students know and do not know. Junk them!

Last, fill-in-the-blank questions are inane. They really pose the question from teacher to student, "Guess what I am thinking; bet you don't know!" It is a guessing game, not a measuring device, to find if students have learned material.

I would not have taken the time to mention these (true-false, matching, and fill-in-the-blank), but I continue to see them on teacher tests, as sad as it seems. They even show up in textbooks at the close of chapters. The only worthwhile objective questions are multiple choice, and these have to be carefully crafted to serve the purpose of answering the desired question How Will I Know I've Arrived? For instance, a good multiple-choice question possesses some givens: Of the five possible answers, two are easily seen as wrong by a student who has learned the material. A third choice is enough off base, but not totally, that the same student realizes without too much study that it is wrong. Of the two remaining choices, one is close but detectably incorrect, and the other is on the mark, that is, correct. Such questions and choices are not easy to construct, so when a teacher comes up with a winner, keep it. The question itself must be clear, concise, and understandable to the conscientious student in the first reading. It also must measure what the teacher desires. Important! For a short course on multiple-choice question construction, consult the *Taxonomy of Educational Objectives: Cognitive Domain* (1956). Benjamin Bloom edited this famous, but mostly unused, yet valuable book. Among many in the book, an excellently constructed question and five choices, for example, is on page 151. That example of an intelligently worded multiple-choice question (with choices like the ones I discussed a little earlier) illustrates its value to a teacher. She quickly discovers her students' various abilities to analyze the elements of an argument, which is a high-order thinking skill. If she has first pre-tested such abilities then has taught them how to do this (analyze elements of an argument), and they are successful on a test with such questions as the one referred to above, her teaching success is obvious.

Finally, she has not had to spend hours and hours laboring over more subjective student responses to short-answer or essay questions that measure the same thing. Thus, it is worth spending time creating multiple-choice questions when the results measure what teachers want to measure (validity). Therefore, teachers know they have arrived at the proper destination.

Caution! Do not use multiple-choice questions, no matter how well constructed and valid, to the exclusion of short-answer essay questions. It is every teacher's responsibility to teach youngsters to write as well as to ponder, and the disciplines of math, science, industrial technology, business, languages of other countries, social studies, and physical fitness offer excellent opportunities for teachers to accomplish this.

To hone the skills necessary to use analysis, synthesis, and evaluation (the top three critical thinking skills), every pedagogue from grade school through high school goes beyond multiple-choice questions at least occasionally to teach and test writing and speaking. Why every teacher? Because these are the skills everyone uses in life to communicate one's ability to analyze, synthesize, and evaluate. Granted, such practice increases teacher time on the job, but unless all do it, students do not exit school able to express themselves convincingly and grammatically in writing and speaking. All teachers are college graduates, so all are literate and articulate enough to do it. Naturally, this practice cuts the amount of subject matter taught each year, but there is much in *How Shall I Get There?* as pointed out in the last chapter, that should be eliminated anyway. Once schools adopt the practice of teaching and measuring writing and speaking skills across the curriculum, American students stand above most of their contemporaries in other parts of the world.

How will I know I've arrived? Eliminate all true-false, matching, and fill-in-the-blank questions. Substitute painstakingly constructed and valid multiple-choice questions with the kinds of choices I discussed earlier in the chapter, and teach and measure across the curriculum students' abilities to write and speak convincingly and grammatically. Teachers not only arrive then, they arrive at the proper destination with feelings of satiety and gratification.

CONCLUSION

Chapter 6 takes the reader to the first of the ten assumptions that must be met to make STAR Theory a reality. The subject matter of chapter 6 implies work, but more than that, it implies fun, a genetic need to remain sane on our spinning planet. When teachers who have *it* assist those who want *it,* the fun begins. Keep in mind that transferring the *it* requires continued education, disciplined practice, support from others, and time—lots and lots of time! But, the resulting joy permeates the whole community of teachers, learners, administrators, parents, patrons, and even the bystanders.

CHAPTER 6

Assumption Number 1

A MAJORITY OF SUCCESSFUL TEACHERS IS
RESIDENT IN THE DISTRICT, AND THE MAJORITY
MENTORS THE MINORITY

A district wishing to implement STAR Theory works diligently to employ those who fit the description of successful teachers detailed in earlier chapters. Sometimes district personnel employ those who do not quite meet the description because of inexperience or previous less-than-appropriate training programs. The district then provides success-ful trainers (resident successful teachers) for them until they reach that level. It is important that this training is intense before the trainees achieve tenure. In such a short time, it is difficult to achieve soundness in pedagogy with fairly inexperienced teachers, but if they are on the STAR Theory path, little doubt exists about their eventually reaching the goal. What does ". . . if they are on the STAR Theory path . . ." mean? Important question, but the answer is even more important, and here it is: (1) They exhibit wholesome attitudes toward their students by consistently developing and maintaining caring relationships with all of them, not just the "pleasant" ones; (2) they learn to teach stu-dents responsible behavior after each instance of rejecting an irrespon-sible act or expression; (3) they show continuing, positive growth in pedagogy; (4) they cause most of their students to exit at least compe-tent in relevant subject matter and responsible in citizenship.

In the beginning of the school year immediately following employ-ment of teachers, the supervising principals pay close attention to num-bers 1 and 2. In the teachers' classes during the first month and a half, the supervisor soon discovers whether the new hires are the right ones as the supervisor observes the teachers (1) developing caring relation-ships with *all* students, and (2) consistently rejecting irresponsible

student acts and expressions, then teaching responsible behavior immediately.

School leaders in charge of deciding tenure work closely with
teacher trainers and trainees before making such important decisions.
Because this and the nine remaining assumptions are met when realizing the fruits of STAR Theory, here is that theory again:

> Sound in pedagogy, the successful teacher creates and maintains a caring
> relationship with all students, rejects their acts and expressions of irre-
> sponsibility and teaches them responsibility. Ultimately, almost all, if
> not all, the successful teacher's charges exit competent or better in rele-
> vant subject matter and responsible in citizenship.

With enough successful teachers on the job in the district teaching
corps, an ongoing training program exists at all schools. Each school
principal assigns one or more new hires to a resident successful
teacher. The new hires, in signing contracts, have agreed to work to
meet the requirements of STAR Theory. The training program each
successful teacher implements remains in effect until the trainees
become successful teachers, according to the trainer and the supervising principal who work jointly to make this happen. The supervising
principal has no job priorities higher than the one to help successful
teachers implement the training program and to stay close enough to
what is happening that the principal, with myriad classroom visits and
with the trainer's input, extends or does not extend tenure to the
trainee.

Of course, districts serious about implementing the training program
do so long before a majority of their district's teachers meet the STAR
Theory description, assuming that is the status in some districts. The
theory has little chance of achieving its purpose before more than half
the district's pedagogues are successful. Why? It is almost impossible
to overcome the myriad student attitudes, behaviors, and even habits
inculcated by less-than-successful teachers when these folks number
half or more of the district teacher corps. Also, other assumptions tie
into this one, and all are met before the theory has a chance to work
well. If one doubts this, just look at the many school districts across the
nation in which only a few schools of excellence are named by a blue-
ribbon panel. There also is a much better chance for a school of excellence at the elementary level to be truly a successful school than one
named so at the high school level. The true school of excellence at the

high school level must be fed by elementary and middle or junior high schools with majorities of successful teachers and leaders and located in areas where more than half the patrons embrace the district's and their schools' missions; otherwise, the current epithet "School of Excellence" for the high school is only a pipe dream. Think not? Check on these schools' drop-outs and graduates who exit less than competent in relevant subject matter and less than responsible in citizenship. In STAR Theory, remember, " . . . almost all, if not all, their students exit competent or better in relevant subject matter and responsible in citizenship." Quite a difference exists between a blue-ribbon school and a STAR Theory school, at least at the middle and high school levels.

The bottom line is that an exemplary elementary school leader and an exemplary staff have a whale of a lot better chance to develop a successful school than those who labor in the secondary schools. Even so, the exemplary elementary school principal and staff work tirelessly to get a majority of their parents and patrons to embrace the school mission through the years before success reaches fruition. School personnel do not accomplish this without that support. Remember the aphorism, "It takes a village to rear a child?" Well, it takes a majority of the parents and patrons in the attendance area to subscribe to and embrace an elementary school's mission (when that school is staffed with a plethora of successful teachers and a successful principal) to make a successful school. This is why the key to any school district's success is an exemplary elementary school program. Without such an elementary school program in the district, forget about achieving excellence or success for almost all, if not all, the youngsters as they matriculate in the middle, junior, and senior high schools in the district.

Successful teachers need recognition as the real STARs of schools in the United States, and the school leaders, above all others, help teachers shine more brightly. But, the star schools in the United States are first, the elementary schools; those schools and their leaders are pivotal in producing successful Americans. Former Commissioner of Education John Gardner, one of the unsung heroes in the history of our nation's public education, once said something close to the following: A nation is not measured by its leaders doing extraordinary things; a nation is measured by its citizens doing ordinary things extraordinarily well. I follow Gardner's lead with this: The educational journey begins in utero. During those nine months, the five years following in the (it is hoped) loving home, and during the first five or six years of formal schooling, more good, sound, glorious things can happen to cause the U.S. citizenry to excel in extraordinary ways, than during any other period in people's lives.

According to some, a piece of Benjamin Bloom research is one of the most powerful studies in the twentieth century. Among other findings, Bloom discovered that half of a child's total intelligence develops during the first four years of life. This was a finding, not a law like Newton's Laws of Gravity. Assuming that Bloom was at least partially correct, the next four, five, or six years are crucial in developing human beings' total intelligence and dispositions toward learning.

EMPLOYING GOOD TEACHERS

Margaret Mead was considered by many to be one of the best teachers in the United States during her sojourn on this planet. After I read her *Coming of Age in Samoa* in graduate school, I tried to read everything this great lady wrote. But an article by Mead that I read thirty years ago had the biggest effect on me. Toward the close of the article, she described good teachers. I do not have the article, but I can paraphrase her description.

> All good teachers have some characteristics in common. The most extraordinary thing about a really good teacher is that s/he transcends accepted educational methods. Such methods are to help the average teacher approximate the performance of a good teacher.
>
> Good teachers want their students, at whatever stage, to learn what it is their task to teach. They are willing to put up with those who are brighter than they are, and there will be some. They are also patient with those who are slower. Their enjoyment of teaching affects those who are taught so they feel some positive emotions—joy, delight, achievement, relief—when they learn what their teachers teach.
>
> Good teachers are always glad when a school year begins and a little sad when it ends. They remember some of their students many years, and their students remember them. They never make assumptions about what their students know or what they can do. They take the trouble to find out, and they are tireless in finding new ways of re-teaching when re-teaching is necessary. In a sense, good teachers always suffer fools gladly.

Margaret Mead's beautiful description of a good teacher is worthy of framing for the wall of every classroom in a successful teacher's environs. It is a description I have given thousands of teachers in the Midwest. It is worthy, also, of distributing to all teachers entering a district determined to graduate virtually all its students competent or better in relevant subject matter and responsible in citizenship. Each school leader in such districts makes it a priority to help every teacher in the school achieve that which Mead has described so ably.

But there is more to it than giving teachers that magnificent statement. New hires enter with an understanding that they achieve success as detailed in the thesis of this book. To enhance such an understanding, interviewers of prospective, and it is hoped, future successful teachers, use an instrument that explains some of these expectations in more detail. Here is one to consider:

For those considering the STAR's role

On a scale of 1 (a quite unhappy person) to 10 (a quite happy person), friends rank me about: _____

I view a glass half full, not half empty. My friends agree with my assessment.

Communicating positively and in a timely fashion with parents is vital. I see them and students as my customers/clients.

Working within the big picture is a must for teamwork and for overall growth.

Securing a master's degree or more in the near future is a goal of mine. Timetable?

Involving students *other than by listening to me* is my main teaching style. Here are examples:

Class management is a strength of mine.

Flexibility is vital to successful teaching.

I listen to, take seriously, and affirm as significant all students.

Staying current with teaching/learning research is necessary. Here's how I do it:

Re-teaching/re-examining students who fall short of competency on occasion is essential to their success.

Implementing team learning often, I satisfy more of my students' basic needs. Examples:

I prepared to teach primarily because I enjoy relating to young people and helping them learn.

Providing for individual differences among students is a must. Examples?

I see principals as advisers, not as ones who administer consequences to students from my class.

Here are some effective logical/natural consequences for student
transgressions in my class.

I conduct class meetings regularly.

I enjoy school activities and shall attend/take part in many during
the school year.

I enjoy good health, am reliable, keep accurate records, and meet
deadlines consistently.

In the presence of students, I control my temper and do not use pro-
fanity.

Please read STAR Theory (including its assumptions) and candidly
discuss your reactions.

In light of the above, I can thrive and live happily here:

(signature)

(date)

"The mightiest powers by deepest calms are fed."

—Barry Cornwall

(Many years ago, a colleague, Dr. Larry Cornine, and I developed the original of this
instrument.)

Why do we not spend more time on the most important decisions
we make—employing outstanding or potentially outstanding teachers?
Next, why do we not spend even more time helping teachers grow in
all the right ways? First question first: School leaders are generally
busy, busy people. Too often, they busy themselves with things that
have deadlines, inanimate things, items that are countable, and so on.
It is true that as time has passed, paper work has proliferated. At first,
we thought computers would lessen the paper in our lives. Not so. What
to do? If you are a school leader, study this instrument and tailor it to
your needs, but please, spend considerable time deciding who teaches
the youngsters. If you are a teacher, a parent, or someone else who
cares a great deal about student competence and good citizenship, show
this to a principal or to a superintendent. Glasser said that teaching is
the toughest job on the planet. I disagree. *Successful* teaching is the
toughest job on the planet, but it is also one of the most intrinsically
rewarding.

When leaders interview prospective teachers, remember it is a two-way street; using an instrument for discussion is the fair way to conduct interviews. The prospects see what is expected. If they agree with the statements on the instrument used for discussion, ask them to sign it. The instrument has some items that are useful when classroom supervision arrives. Use it again when supervisor and teacher get together to discuss teacher progress. School leaders' most important task, after employing their teachers, is working with teachers to help them grow in all the right ways.

Do not let a potentially successful candidate depart without meeting some of the school's successful teachers. Then get a reading from these teachers about the candidate. Several heads are smarter than one. Ask the successful teachers what they think!

HELPING THE NEW STARS SHINE

Do not wait until the school year begins or until visiting classes to assist new hires. Write and say you'll treat them to lunch when they come in during the summer to check on materials, classrooms, and all the other things that go with planning ahead. Invite each new hire's trainer to that lunch. Do not pepper new hires with questions in the summer. Instead, ask them to ask you and the trainer anything they wish to know at that time. Actually, you and the trainer (a successful teacher) can learn much about the new troops using that modus operandi.

Toward summer's closing weeks, send an official welcome with a schedule of weekly breakfast meetings during the first month of school. Ask the trainers to write welcome letters to their trainees mentioning a pre-school workshop meeting of trainees, trainers, and the school's leaders. The pre-school meeting is a time to answer more trainee interrogatives and to go over the minutiae peculiar to beginning school. Important: Let every new hire know that no question is stupid.

At this pre-school meeting of trainees, trainers, and school leaders, cite expectations in major areas, such as trainers and trainees getting together for regular confabs, free lunches for trainees and trainers during the first week of school with trainers ensuring that trainees have escorts through the lunch lines, and finally, the modus operandi of school leaders' supervision and evaluation of trainees (make certain each trainee has a copy of the official final evaluation instrument at that time).

Prior to the first day of school, place some warm fuzzies in trainees' mailboxes, such as packs of chewing gum or mints and personal notes from the school leaders with appropriate aphorisms, and so on.

Supervising principals (school leaders) should visit trainees' classes every school day the first month, but take no paper or pen. However, if good pedagogy and/or positive relationships with students are resident, write brief notes (when returning to the offices) to that effect and place these in the trainees' boxes. Be a caring professional!

At the weekly inservice breakfast meetings, principals answer trainees' questions about things that perplex them. Reminder: No comment or question is stupid. During the next-to-last breakfast, the principal distributes a lesson plan for the last breakfast, the principal's turn to teach. Principals, knock 'em dead at the final morning meal! Among other things, let trainees know the supervising principals start visiting classes for real during the second month. Supervising principals visit new hires at least every other school day the next month with an appropriate epistle placed in each new hire's box following a visit. Follow each visit with a brief confab to answer trainees' questions about the letter.

It is amazing that so many school leaders believe they can adequately evaluate a teacher with one or two classroom visits *per year!* That is not caring, not professional. If you re-read the past couple of paragraphs, it is apparent that each trainee's supervising principal is in the trainee's classroom about thirty times or more the first couple of months. Tell me, please, what is more important in school leaders' days, weeks, and months of a school year than spending time where the action is, where the STARs meet the customers (students)? Answer: *nothing!* And such leader presence does not stop after the second month. Every day, exemplary school leaders visit almost all school classrooms. At the close of a school year, if a district patron asks a teacher from any district school how often the school leader comes into the classroom during the year, teachers in successful schools matter-of-factly respond, "Oh, just about every day when s/he is not attending meetings elsewhere."

Back to collaboration: Supervising principals and trainers get together often during the first two months to confer about trainees' needs. Remember, trainers are not evaluators; they are user-friendly mentors.

Supervising principals send new hires "Happy Birthday" notes during the school year with an attached free-lunch ticket. If birthdays are in the summer, send these notes the last week of the school year with the attached lunch ticket good that week or the first week of the next school year.

A school leader involves new hires in school activities, but does not overdo it. Such involvement gives new hires a positive look at school life before/after the school day. Meet with all trainees toward the middle of or in late January to solicit questions about how to improve what the school leaders do to help new hires' first months more enjoyable and fruitful. Another breakfast meeting is a good venue, and again, breakfasts are free to new hires and trainers.

Remind each trainee to visit not only the trainer's classes but other successful teachers' classes as well. The supervising principal is happy to pinch-hit in class while the trainee does this. The principal suggests the names of successful teachers to visit.

Give every new hire an abbreviated copy of *A Message to Garcia* (Hubbard 1899) at the close of the first year at a final breakfast meeting. Remind new hires that the reason they receive copies is for them to help enable every youngster to deliver the message to Garcia. A later chapter has more about this and a recommended short version for the school leader to read aloud at this time. This is one of the most powerful stories a leader shares at the close of year number one.

During the second year, repeat many kindnesses and meet often with second-year teachers. Remember that too many potentially good teachers leave the profession the first few years of teaching. ENCOURAGE! ENCOURAGE! ENCOURAGE!

Shakespeare wrote something like the following (sexist language changed): What a piece of work is a human being! how noble in reason! how infinite in faculty! in form and moving how express and admirable! in action how like an angel! in apprehension how like a god! the beauty of the world! the paragon of animals!

TRAINER AND TRAINEE

The trainer is a successful teacher as described in STAR Theory, and every successful teacher has a unique style in achieving success. However, just because trainers are already successful teachers of young people, it might not follow that they are such with adults. Thus, the school leader spends a great deal of time with trainers in individual and group dialogues. From the first meeting, the school leader makes clear to the trainers that their task is not supervisory or evaluative. Their task is to help teach the new hires how to become successful teachers, powerful challenges to all trainers.

If the trainer and new hire do not mesh, and this does happen without anyone to blame, encourage both the new hire and the trainer to recognize this and ask the supervising principal to find a different trainer. Let nothing stand in the way of trainees reaching success.

It is hoped the school has a budget for assisting trainers to work with trainees. It should include a stipend for each trainer and funds for other things that enhance the growth of trainees. Such things might include unforeseen educational materials that surface during a particular year, such as attendance at professional conferences, an occasional weekend or holiday working-breakfast that a trainer and the trainee decide they need to solve a problem or discuss an idea at length away from the madding crowd. Successful schools are places where growth is a constant, not a sporadic, phenomenon. Professionals deserve budgets to encourage and to serve these phenomena.

CONCLUSION

As the reader goes to assumption number 2 in chapter 7, the important concept of teamwork is discernible there, also. Without cooperation between the central office leaders and the school leaders, the former may not see the need to practice STAR Theory with those they lead. If everyone on board is not fully informed about the theory and practices, STAR Theory, like any other theory, simply fails to work.

Before any district even seriously considers implementing something like these changes, a completely thought-out inservice program must be in place. Whether that program thrives or flounders depends on the leaders at each level, individually and collectively. Effective leaders seldom, if ever, flounder!

CHAPTER 7

Assumption Number 2

SCHOOL AND CENTRAL OFFICE LEADERS PRACTICE STAR THEORY WITH THOSE THEY LEAD

This chapter first examines how school leaders exemplify STAR Theory. Second, central office leadership appears under the microscope in a similar way. Finally, we look at the relationship of school and central office leaders to one another, one of many crucial relationships in making the theory or, for that matter, any school district work well. Teamwork among people throughout a district practicing this theory is a key to success. A fourth grader once asked the person with the highest IQ on the planet, "What is the greatest thing people have done?" Marilyn vos Savant replied, "The greatest thing people have ever done is decide to cooperate. Cooperation was the most important element in conquering smallpox, traveling to the moon, and achieving any peace that has lasted." Cooperation is also the most important element in making schools work the right way for youngsters.

Please keep in mind, however, that the chief function of school leaders and before them, the district person in charge of employing teachers, is to find successful teachers. The next most important function of school leaders is to help resident successful teachers develop other successful teachers in the schools. All else pales in comparison with these functions! The superintendent's chief function (or that of the superintendent's delegated human resource leader) is to find and employ successful school leaders, individuals who are former STARs with students in classrooms; thus, they know classroom STARs when they find them. If every facet of this paragraph's vital information is followed to the letter, district students eventually exit at least competent in relevant subject matter and responsible in citizenship. Why else do schools exist?

THE IMPORTANCE OF MODELING BY SCHOOL LEADERS

Cooperation is the launching pad for the journey, the engine that keeps everyone on the same page, and the glue that binds us as we sail together toward Ithaca. Thus, unless school leaders cooperate with those they lead by modeling STAR Theory, it won't be long before teachers decide that the theory is a sham and not worth the effort. So, how do leaders at the school level model the theory?

Modeling is not a new idea. Parents who want their children to behave as model citizens simply behave as model citizens behave. In essence, they ask their children to do as they do, and then what they say makes sense. However, when parents yell at or beat their children, they are sending the message, "It is all right to yell at and to beat people." Such behavior leads to black eyes and, often, to prison.

When school leaders, principals, for example, offer to pinch-hit in classrooms for teachers and follow by modeling sound pedagogy, rejecting student acts and expressions of irresponsibility, and teaching the transgressors responsibility, they are modeling STAR Theory for the teachers they lead.

If the school mission is to listen to, take seriously, affirm as significant, and improve the quality of life of all our students, then every act and expression emanating from school leaders' beings model that mission. For instance, such school leaders take the time to listen to the people in the community when these people ask for audiences. In such settings, these leaders take seriously what the people say, and they follow by affirming all as significant human beings even when they disagree with what they say. Often, such conversations are delayed, and some never need to take place because effective school leaders refer complaints about teachers to the source—the teachers themselves.

Here is a prime example: Jeannie goes home from school and at the dinner table she discusses school that day. She says excitedly, "Mommie, Daddy, guess what we did at school today!" Then, Jeannie tells her parents something that upsets them greatly. The next day, either Mother or Dad, still upset, calls the principal and reports what Jeannie has said happened in class yesterday.

The principal listens to the parent carefully and calmly, showing by her response that she takes the parent seriously. She then affirms the parent as significant by saying something like, "Do you know, Mr(s). Barton, I realize you'd like to check this whole thing out with the source, so why don't I ask Jeannie's teacher, Mrs. Horner, to call you, or if you'd rather come on up to school and talk with her, I'd be glad to teach her class while you and Mrs. Horner talk in my office, whichever is convenient for you. Then, if after you two talk either by phone or here in person, if you'd like to discuss it further with me, I'll make myself available at your convenience. How does that sound to you?"

This conversation might be fictional, but it and thousands of telephone conversations similar to it have taken place in many schools. In fact, I have been a part of more than a few of those conversations. When the teacher talks with the upset parent, the teachers also listens to, takes seriously, and affirms the parent as significant. In my fifty years as an educator, the teacher and the parent who conduct such a dialogue almost always part company in a friendly manner. Why? Because the Jeannies who report to their parents almost always leave something out, or don't explain what happened entirely accurately, not intentionally, but humanly.

Here's a valuable piece of advice I have given thousands of teachers: Everything you say or do in class could end up at the dinner table that evening, so remember two important things: Think things through before you say or do them, and if what you say or do could be misunderstood, write it on paper and give it to the students.

So, school leaders model the school mission to the letter, model their own missions, and model STAR Theory. The perfect way for a school leader to model the theory is to conduct staff meetings in the manner that a successful teacher conducts classes. In other words, staff meetings are exciting only when those present learn things useful, presented in animated ways. For example, many years ago I read Gore Vidal's wonderful historical novel *Lincoln* (1984), and it occurred to me that one of our Oak Park teachers, Roy Williams, might be willing to play the part of Lincoln delivering one of the greatest speeches ever rendered, the Gettysburg Address, at our two February staff meetings.

Roy was Lincolnesque in build and demeanor—almost six feet, four inches tall, thin, bearded, intense (although not at all pompous), and witty, so the staff would see him as a natural. I told Roy about Vidal's book, and my idea to set up his entrance to the meeting: "All of us can make our subjects live by inviting great figures from the past to our classrooms, people like Einstein, Sir Isaac Newton, Clara Barton, Emily Dickinson, Pythagoras, the list is endless. By doing so, we show our students that learning is real, albeit sometimes we present it fictionally. Tomorrow, for instance, is Abraham Lincoln's 171st birthday, and because we live in an age of technology, we are able to do things undreamed of earlier in this century and before. Today, we are able and shall bring to the present one of the world's greatest human beings who has consented to share with us—the staff at this school—one of the greatest speeches of all time, the one he delivered almost 117 years ago in a small town in south-central Pennsylvania. Ladies and gentlemen of one of the world's great schools, please help me welcome to the Main Theatre of Oak Park, the sixteenth president of the United States, one of the most influential figures of human history, Mr. Abraham Lincoln."

Roy consented and accepted the script, which consisted of two or three pages of Vidal's book that included the writer's stirring narration and Lincoln's rendering of the Gettysburg Address. We agreed to rehearse a couple of times before the two performances, and Roy found suitable clothing, including a stovepipe hat, string tie, old spectacles, and a black suit for the two meetings. I agreed to read Vidal's narration from the background, and we asked Head Custodian Jim Lawrence to set up a small stage of risers in the pit in front of the Main Theatre stage.

When I introduced Roy as Lincoln, we had a student lower the house lights and another shine a spotlight on the stage and follow Roy as he walked out from the wing of the stage, down the steps, and onto the small stage in the pit. The silence in the audience was total, and as I began the narration, all eyes were riveted on "Mr. Lincoln."

Following Roy's superb rendering of the 262 words of the Gettysburg Address, the house lights went up, the spotlight off, and I said, "Ladies and gentlemen, the sixteenth president of the United States, Mr. Abraham Lincoln."

The applause was spontaneous and long. Then, I said, "Mr. President, would you be kind enough to join us for a few minutes while I close the meeting because I am certain, sir, that many of our teachers want an opportunity to visit a moment or two with you?"

Roy (Mr. Lincoln) nodded, went down the two steps, walked over to the front row and seated himself among the teachers. I quickly adjourned the meeting, and the multitudes rushed to shake "Mr. Lincoln's" hand and congratulate him. It was a surreal feeling, I was told by many.

Roy repeated the performance the next morning at the 6:45 a.m. meeting, and it was just as spellbinding as the day before even though a few had heard about it from friends who had attended the afternoon meeting. I repeated this meeting when I was the interim principal at another school in the district, and that time had it videotaped.

When a leader plans staff meetings for the school year, often it is wise to have a theme and follow the theme at each of the meetings the way teachers follow organized lesson plans. However, the main consideration is planning each meeting with sound pedagogy in mind. Most school leaders have been teachers who have made myriad lesson plans to use in teaching youngsters. The chief differences for a principal working with staff members rather than with students:

1. The setting is now filled with licensed pedagogues whose goals are primarily to lead youngsters to excellence in relevant subject matter and to responsibility in citizenship, so treat them accordingly.
2. They have either taught all day or have risen early to attend a morning staff meeting the leader has planned.
3. Some will arrive late, so treat them as you did students, with dignity.
4. A few will attend neither scheduled meeting for various reasons, so do the same as you did with the youngsters in your classrooms, seek them out and arrange a mutually convenient time for the absent pedagogues to make up what they missed. Do this, too, with dignity.
5. In light of the preceding, fill each scheduled meeting with vital subject matter for every attendee, as you did when you taught the young.
6. Now—counting pre-school workshop, monthly staff meetings, and a closing meeting or two after the students' school year ends—a dozen or fewer lesson plans to create (yes, create), so create exemplary ones!

Teachers should keep in mind each time a school leader calls a meeting that the leader is the resident expert in pedagogy, not simply a bean counter, a supervisor, an organizer, or a consequence dispenser. In the setting of meetings, the leader is a presenter, an involver of those present, an active listener, an initiator, a servant to those present, and one who follows up on the results of those meetings.

The first few pages of this chapter contain examples of modeling STAR Theory and exemplary leadership at the school leader level. Readers, for certain, are able to expand on these, but as they do, please consider carefully that the leader's primary challenge is to help the school's STARs—successful teachers—shine more brightly.

MODELING BY CENTRAL OFFICE LEADERS

Here is a radical, but wonder-filled idea to help the school district personnel come together as a cohesive team with each member understanding better why successful teachers are the STARs of each educational community, and why successful teachers have the toughest job on the planet: Start modestly by asking each certified staff member in the district who is not a full-time classroom teacher to sub for a classroom teacher one day a month. With good pre-planning of this venture, and with excellent preparation and communication between those subbing one day a month and the classroom teachers for whom they are subbing, the venture could grow into twice a month the second year, and who knows what after that.

Central office leaders, too, model STAR Theory every day on the job while in and out of the presence of those they lead. For instance, they work with people they lead the way STAR teachers work with their students. They develop and maintain caring relationships with those they lead, reject acts and expressions of irresponsibility and teach them responsibility. The accent here is on *teach*. Many central office leaders do not believe it is their job to teach responsibility to those they lead. They say to themselves, "They're adults; they should know how to behave responsibly." Not always so! While maintaining the caring relationship, the leader humanely, kindly, and patiently teaches responsibility to those who have behaved irresponsibly or who have, for whatever reason, expressed themselves irresponsibly.

Let's take an example: A bus driver loses his cool and cusses out a student who has been irresponsible on the bus. The student (or the parent) complains to the director of transportation, Mr. Smith, who says, "Please, let me get back to you after I visit with Mr. Brown" (bus driver). The director visits with Brown and finds that he has cooled off since the incident happened. Smith asks the driver what he thinks is a solution to the problem.

Brown says, "I should have handled it differently. I simply should have written the kid up on the form provided, explaining exactly what happened, and then I should have turned in the slip to the principal. The kid was rude, got under my skin, and I lost it!"

Smith says, "We all lose it at times and grow wiser from our mistakes. What would you suggest as a solution, Bill?"

Brown says, "Let me apologize to the kid for blowing it, and tell him because I blew it, he can ride the bus tomorrow, and if I hadn't lost it, and had just filled out the misbehavior form, he'd have been off the bus for a week. Then, following my apology and that statement, I'll offer to shake hands with him and smile. What do you think?"

Smith says, "That's a great idea and a maturely thought-out solution. I do believe you've solved the problem."

In the preceding example, through his deft handling of the problem, the director gave the driver the opportunity to teach himself responsible behavior, and he did. This often works with students and with adults.

SCHOOL AND CENTRAL OFFICE RELATIONSHIPS

When central office personnel begin pinch-hitting as teachers in the district schools, this is a perfect time for them and the school leaders to relate. For instance, the instructional leader spends a great deal of time in classrooms. Why not drop in on central office pinch-hitters in the classroom and take them to lunch. What a wonderful opportunity to exchange ideas and to chat. No better avenue exists for relationships than the dining table.

However, make certain you do this in the two different school venues for dining—the student cafeteria and the staff dining area if there is one. Sit with students often as you chat, drawing them into the conversations. Ask them for ideas about how to make their school an even better place. And, see if you can entice the central office leader to explain what she does for a living in supporting the district's successful teachers, its STARs.

Another great venue for developing relationships is in the staff dining area where central office gurus and school staff can interact and learn more about each other's work and lives. It's quite humanizing.

Modeling STAR Theory, school leaders invite central office leaders to staff meetings before and after school occasionally. Even ask them to take part in a meeting in some important way. Remember, we value most what we contribute to and value least what we are not part of. Also, if schools have shared decision-making meetings at the school site, invite central office leaders to these confabs.

CONCLUSION

Finally, follow the Latin assertion, *carpe diem!* Seize the moment any time an opportunity exists for interaction with dialogue and cooperation, for such opportunities lead to positive growth.

The next chapter contains one of the most important conditions in this book because it is about a problem that has been increasing in severity the past three decades. Poor student attendance must become a relic of the past if every student is to exit at least competent in relevant subject matter and responsible in citizenship.

CHAPTER 8

Assumption Number 3

STUDENTS ATTEND SCHOOL REGULARLY

The largest single deterrent to student achievement in U.S. schools is poor attendance. It always has been, but it is not necessarily always going to be. The day might come when everyone does not need to attend regularly to achieve, but the way we organize and administer most schools today, regular student attendance is necessary. Even when and if that day arrives, students must understand the requirements for achievement and make the effort to meet those requirements wherever circumstances place them. With stakeholders working together in STAR Theory, however, poor student attendance is something out of the past.

A LITTLE HISTORY

In years of yore, an agrarian economy determined the school year, so the fall term began when parents on the farms could literally afford to have their progeny absent from home duties. Even then, Father and Mother kept their youngsters home when they needed them during the school year to perform tasks that made a difference in whether the family survived economically. First things first, they called it, and schoolmasters did not argue because many of them also lived on farms. Teaching was often a second job for teachers.

In those days, parents and children talked and collaborated several hours every day and evening. Parents and their children shared the same values and culture. The vast majority stopped the formal schooling process at eighth grade to serve as full-time workers on the family farms.

After World War II, grown children returned as adults to the cities and territories around the cities rather than to the family farms. The GI Bill was partially the cause, because those who had never considered college now had means to go. Many said that the GI Bill changed the face of the nation. Right or wrong, the United States eventually coined a new word, *suburbs.*

During the war, women left the home and took the places of the men who had gone off to war. Rosie the Riveter was born, and she did not go back to the life she had led in the 1930s and early 1940s. No longer living in an agrarian economy, Rosie and millions more men and women earned their bread and butter in the cities and suburbs. It took a few years, but now, for the first time in U.S. history, parents and children began developing different values and cultures. Why?

Simple answer. They did not spend as much time together as they used to, so they went their separate ways, doing their own things. Remember, this happened gradually following World War II. Before the war, one or more extended relatives lived with Mom, Dad, and the kids under the same roof in well more than half of American homes. When our young returned from war, mainly to the cities and suburbs, married and then had children, this all changed. Whereas before, there was almost always an adult around to talk and collaborate with the young adults and continue the family values and culture, in the late 1940s and 1950s, these new moms and dads had to go it alone with their kids.

Whom did the youngsters turn to for collaboration and dialogue to make judgments, form values, and think critically? They turned to their friends for advice in these sensitive and complex domains, friends who knew no more than they did about making sound judgments, thinking critically, or forming wholesome values. This led eventually to gangs. Why?

Gang membership satisfied genetic needs (Glasser 1992) not met in the home: the need to belong, feel important, experience freedom, and have fun. Youngsters began spending more time with their friends than with their parents, so they adopted the values and culture of their friends. Sadly, the lack of maturity in forming these values led often to violence and other untoward behaviors. However, another phenomenon surfaced shortly after the war, and eventually, most Americans had access to it—*television.*

Television has always had many pluses, but unmonitored and without mature adults present to discuss the programs with, the young found the minuses prevailing in value formation, in thinking critically, and in making sound judgments. Television caused the world to shrink even more than airplanes did. In the past, and that refers to all of history, families shared values in music. They used to sit around fires to share and enjoy ceremonial music and dances. Later, families shared in the leisure of live musical groups. When radio came, it was more usual than unusual for families to sit around the radio many evenings and on Saturday nights and listen to shows like *Hit Parade* and many other programs with live music.

When Dick Clark and his *American Bandstand,* and a little later, Elvis and the Beatles, stormed the television airwaves, it was not long before Mom and Dad needed separate sets to watch their stars and listen to their music in the persons of Dinah Shore, Nat Cole, Frank Sinatra, and others. Today, it's MTV and live hard rock concerts for the youngsters, and quiet nights at home or dinner and a movie out for the dads and mothers. At home also these days, many of the young have their own television sets, their own telephones (and cell phones), and an entirely different culture visibly displayed on their walls and furniture.

Fast foods, fast automobiles, a new world of technology, jobs for the young during the school year that cause advertisers to focus a great deal on that important part of the economy, telephones in their rooms and cell phones when away, weekend parties, begin a list that continues nonstop, a list that divides the young from the adult world. All this has increased the competition with school for time and attention in young people's schedules and priorities. Ask any high school principal today, who remembers attendance figures thirty years ago, the following question: Has the average in student attendance dropped during those years and if so, how much? My guess is that most will say it has dropped 5 to 8 percent, and much more in the city schools. And, almost all student failures are attributable to lack of attendance. If they are not present, how can they achieve?

What do we do? Holler "Uncle?" Or do we call the team together, and say, "Whoa! We're not going to take it any more." If your answer is like mine, the latter, let's decide who makes up our team. My immediate suggestion is, "All the stakeholders."

THE STAKEHOLDERS

Who are the stakeholders in U.S. schools? Schools cannot exist without students, so add them to the list. Certainly, students' parents are crucial and it is hoped, vital stakeholders. Every person who works in the schools is a link to student success, so school employees are stakeholders. Those who influence students directly or indirectly are also stakeholders. We are talking about friends, employers, and relatives who live in and out of the area. Finally, those who live in the school district but who have no direct ties with its students or employees have a stake in the schools for many reasons, one of the most important of which is that the school district's reputation draws or repels what makes the United States thrive—business. So, these folks are stakeholders, too. If we examine each group listed, perhaps we can find ways to increase attendance.

The Students

The school's ace in the hole is to make attendance so appealing that youngsters want to be there. How? When one has studied and practiced sound pedagogy long enough, the answer seems clear and simple: *Involve students more often in the learning process with useful things to learn and organize them into learning teams at least half the time.* When not part of a learning team, students need to listen less and act more. By act, I mean they *do* things other than listen most of the time. Elementary teachers know this, but many secondary teachers have forgotten that telling and teaching are not always synonymous. If they were, we'd be much smarter. Sure, we need to use telling as a teaching method some of the time, but always keep the ancient Chinese proverb on the tip of the teaching tongue: I hear, and I forget; I see, and I remember; I do, and I understand. It's the same as learning to swim, riding a bicycle, and driving a car. Yes, these are motor activities, but intellectual ones also stick better if students *do* them.

For example, we learn the basics of how to read by taking the activity apart, but reading itself takes place only after we practice the basics by doing, that is, by reading. We learn the times tables by putting 5 x 5, 8 x 9, and 4 x 3 in our memory banks, but we do not keep them there if we fail to use them. You still have the times tables through the tens at your age. I have them as a septuagenarian. Why? Because we have used them often through the years. That's doing! Here's another example: I learned in junior high why, when I was sitting in the press box performing analyst duties on radio and television in later life, it took a while for the sound of the marching band's instruments to reach my ears. But I would not have remembered that if, to stay safe, I had not used the information often all these years to count the seconds from the time I saw lightning flash until I heard thunder clap. Sound still travels 1,100 feet per second when the atmosphere is still.

Examples are myriad, but the cliché still applies, use it or lose it! Doing useful things monopolizes the sound pedagogue's teaching activities when her youngsters are not involved in team learning. And, when they are learning in teams involved in worthwhile activities, they are again, doing, and they are also discussing and collaborating.

Families may talk and collaborate fifteen minutes or so a day nowadays, but good teachers make up for this with wholesome learning activities that require talking and collaborating. Teachers, pepper your class sessions with dialogue and collaboration, and good things will happen with your youngsters. With close pedagogue monitoring, they learn to listen and to speak well, and they learn to get along with one another. The *uhs* and the *ands* diminish appreciably in their speech patterns, and with carefully guided practice, they learn to think well, too, because they discuss vital material. What, think?

School is filled with learning—memorizing those things worth memorizing because we use them the rest of our lives. But *thinking*—figuring out what to do when we don't know what to do—is sadly missing from school activities. When I asked teachers many years ago at Oak Park High to increase the number of learning activities using the higher-order thinking skills of analysis, synthesis, and evaluation, Bob Walsh (one of the best teachers I've known), after a semester of diligence said, "Dan, it's like pulling teeth."

Thinking activities need to begin in the lower grades and pervade our schools' curricula through grade twelve. Bloom's *Taxonomy of Educational Objectives: Cognitive Domain* has been used little since it was published in the mid-1950s, but no teacher preparation institution should allow its teachers-to-be to graduate without requiring competence in the use of this book's concepts and practices. Thinking will then enter school classrooms in abundance.

The Parents

Parents of America, unite! Unite, that is, by contributing to, then embracing, the district and school missions where your young people attend school. Implied in every mission worth the paper it's printed on is the following: Students attend school regularly. Now, it is time to discuss the specifics of that statement.

In Missouri a few years ago, the General Assembly passed legislation to encourage the young to continue their formal education beyond high school. It is called the *A+ program*. In the North Kansas City Schools, for instance, all three high schools' students are eligible to take advantage of this powerful program. In addition to maintaining a 2.5 (4.0 scale) grade point average during four years of high school, performing a certain number of hours of community service, maintaining good citizenship, student recipients also *must average 95% attendance through the four years of high school.* If they meet these criteria, those who entered the A+ program as freshmen may enroll in any state-approved community college and attend two years tuition-free.

Attending school 95 percent of the time is STAR Theory's definition of attending school regularly. Let's assume the school year is 180 student-teacher contact days. Take 180 x 4 school years, and the total is 720 days of school. Ninety-five percent of 720 days is 684. That means students may miss 36 school days during four years of high school and still qualify under STAR Theory's definition of those who attend school regularly. Who argues that missing an average of nine school days per year is unreasonable? Hopefully, not many!

As the A+ program becomes common among Missouri high schools, the effect on the economy undoubtedly will be unbelievably positive. Many graduates, of course, forsake community college for four-year institutions, but the majority of those who choose and succeed in the A+ program are those who, otherwise, might not have furthered their formal education, and virtually everyone knows the statistics on high school graduates' earning power and the earning power of those who continue two or more years in college. My recommendation is that all states follow the Missouri A+ program initiative or something similar and begin to change the face of America again, this time with a significant increase in the number of youngsters who continue formal education well beyond the high school diploma. Shades of the old GI Bill!

How will this improve high school attendance significantly? By laying the foundation for those who see that good attendance pays off, and by requiring something more to graduate from high school. Historically, employers have asked high school principals more about the reliability (good attendance) and the citizenship of their graduates than about grades. It is time to require good attendance for high school graduation. In STAR Theory school districts, regular student attendance is a given and is more than implied in the district and school missions. In a later chapter, I discuss how STAR Theory districts expect parents and patrons to embrace the district and school missions. I also articulate a plan to accomplish this in that chapter.

So parents who embrace the district and school missions take advantage of windfalls like the A+ program and make certain that their young people attend school 95 percent of the time.

The School District Staff Members

Naturally, members of the school district staff practice what STAR Theory preaches. Therefore, the superintendent, the various department leaders, the school principals, and the teachers practice and preach exemplary attendance. One preachment is the following: *Reliability is necessary for exemplary performance.* Exemplary performance requires diligence and presence. Diligence means working consistently in right ways to improve task performance. Presence, of course, means being on task regularly. Thus, to perform in an exemplary manner, a reliable staff is diligent and present.

When a staff is reliable and performs well, students observe this every day, and less preaching is necessary. But parameters are in place for students to measure themselves. One of the important measuring sticks is school attendance, and students understand that they must be in attendance at least 95 percent of the time during the school year. Exemplary student achievement presupposes being there 95 percent of the time. This is a given, and no more effective models exist than school staff members who exemplify it.

Direct and Indirect Influences on Students

Unmistakably, friends, relatives, and employers influence youngsters. We discussed the influence of friends earlier, and undeniably, parents and other adults often have less influence during the adolescent years than do friends of adolescents. However, if school teachers and principals call on friends of students who need help making it to school regularly, this source could prove invaluable. As for adult influence, if all who have direct or indirect influences on the young understand that the main way they affect the young is through modeling, they accomplish much by behaving admirably in and out of the young people's presence. School teachers and principals who notice that a student is not attending regularly, should find out who the student's friends and adult influences are and ask for help.

The word that must go out: Remember that you are a model for our young, so behave in ways you wish them to behave when they are your age. Grandparents, perhaps, are in positions to influence their grandchildren more than anyone other than the youngsters' parents and friends. The school is in a good position to let them know this. Communicate with these elder "statespeople" and ask them to stay in touch with their grandchildren's activities. Ask them to write and call and to suggest indirectly that school attendance is vital for school achievement and good habit development. Also, grandparents are often wonderful storytellers. Use them!

Employers are in a unique position to influence the young. Establishing some kind of job reward system for exemplary school attendance does wonders considering how many teenagers work during the school year.

OTHER CITIZENS OF THE DISTRICT

School leaders also communicate the importance of students attending school regularly with the voters of the district who might not currently have direct connections with the young. In turn, these district citizens, when the opportunities arise, communicate with students the impact of exemplary school attendance on happiness and success in the work world, especially if youngsters become involved in the school's self-sustaining activities. They need to tell the young that the school district's reputation tends to be exemplary when youngsters' attendance in school is exemplary.

School leaders also should communicate with these adults in the district that any time they have opportunities to volunteer in the schools, the time spent with the young results in an even stronger, total educational program because these adults affect youngsters in unbelievably positive ways. Many volunteer programs exist. Pam Polson heads Youth Friends in the North Kansas City Schools in Missouri, and it is one of the top-notch volunteer programs in America. Thousands volunteer yearly to help youngsters in myriad ways, and many have no connections with the schools other than through the Youth Friends program. Corporations and companies give such volunteers time off weekly to do this, and senior citizens are part of the program, too.

CONCLUSION

In emphasizing the importance of students attending school at least 95 percent of the time, I reinforce the need for adults to work together in accomplishing the goal. People certainly disagree on many ideas about education, but all surely believe that being present regularly is important in whatever one does. It was called *passing muster* when I was a teenager in the Navy during World War II, and it applied to being at muster many times each day during boot camp and a few months later at battle stations in the South Pacific. We were not there just 95 percent of the time. We were present every moment of every day and night. When muster was called, or the general quarters bell sounded, everyone was present and accounted for!

So it is with school attendance and student achievement. By being there every day, we are more likely to experience happier and more successful tomorrows because people count on our showing up and doing our jobs, whatever those jobs are!

CHAPTER 9

Assumption Number 4

SCHOOLS ARE SMALL

American schools began small and grew larger as the population increased and as people moved away from the agrarian society to suburban and urban societies. It was more economical to build a larger edifice for a school on one plot of ground than to purchase several plots to erect more and smaller schools. However, as school size increased, emphasis on each individual student's needs decreased, although not intentionally. This chapter is about returning to an emphasis on each school youngster by returning to smaller schools and fewer students assigned to teachers (more specifics about the latter at the end of the book). Thus, the residents of such schools and their communities actually know everyone, and everyone knows them—in other words, everybody realistically proclaims, I am truly somebody!

The chapter is in two parts. The first is about school size, how we can decrease the size without purchasing more land on which to build more schools, and why we do this to increase student achievement and improve student citizenship. The second part is about decreasing class size and the total number of students for whom each teacher is responsible. Meeting the conditions of all the assumptions in STAR Theory is important, but meeting the needs of assumption number 4 is crucial if our schools are to be held accountable for improving students' academic achievement and citizenship.

SCHOOL SIZE

Schools can be made smaller without erecting additional buildings. How? Place more than one school in a building. A school, after all, is not the building; it is the unit of people housed in the building. Often, we forget this important concept. Many times I have reminded my graduate students preparing to be principals, directors, and superintendents that no one should ever refer to a leader of a school as a building principal; that is a misnomer. The leader is a school principal just as teachers are school teachers, not building teachers. This is an important point because a school *is* people!

It takes some getting used to, but as long as each school has its own identity through a separate attendance area community, basic program, student body, staff, and administration, there is no reason that more than one school can't occupy a building. Actually, in such an organization, small schools with graduating classes of about 100 students have the additional advantage of offering more options for students. In rural schools, students seldom have the advantage of an enriched curriculum, but in a district with schools that share facilities, many options exist. For example, when two or more schools occupy an elementary school facility, one preschool program and after-school care program is available for more than one school. In secondary schools, if only one high school student body of grades nine through twelve is housed in a facility and the student body numbers about 400 (100 per graduating class), it's expensive to offer math analysis, trig, calculus, physics, and chemistry, drafting III & IV, three foreign languages with upper levels in each, Art II, III, and IV, Drama II, and the list goes on. When STAR Theory is operational, however, four schools of about 400 each are housed in a building that formerly held many more students of one high school. Or, two middle schools of 400 each call home a building that formerly housed 800 in one middle school. This provides advantages that schools within a school enjoyed when they made an appearance in school organization in the 1960s.

The schools-within-a-building-of-schools idea operates like this to great advantage. As long as each school in the building has its own staff in the basic subjects, it is perfectly all right to share staff in areas not ordinarily offered when a small school of 400 is in its own building in a smaller school district. Each school, however, has its own activities program. That way, more youngsters have opportunities to take part in more activities, and according to the research cited earlier, when more students take part in activities, the participating youngsters enhance their chances for success after school days are over.

This is an advantage of the small school. In a high school of 1,600 students, for instance, there is only one varsity football team, one varsity boys basketball team, and one varsity girls basketball team. From the one large school, the four small schools would have a total of four varsity football teams, four boys varsity teams in basketball and four in girls basketball, for example. Far more youngsters take part and excel. The same applies to other activities like debate, drama, music. The 1,600 students in the four small schools have more participants in debate, drama, and music than in the one large school of 1,600 and there are more students outstanding in these activities in the four small schools.

I am not naive, however, about the pressure from parents, patrons, coaches, youngsters, and even the media to keep the large school because, they say, when school enrollment dips to 400, the quality of athletic teams dips, also. How sad this is because many of the athletic teams in four schools of 400 each might be inferior to the athletic teams in a school of 1,600, but the number of girls and boys who participate and excel in the four schools of 400 is far larger than that in the school of 1,600.

In STAR Theory schools, in addition to youngsters enjoying the advantages of sharing staff members in subjects not offered when the four schools of 400 are in four smaller districts, they also benefit when they enroll in orchestra. Whereas each small school within the building has its own modest size marching band, as do schools in smaller districts, in the building housing four schools of 400, music classes unavailable in smaller school districts are available. Let me explain why this is an important point.

When I became a high school principal in a small community of 14,000 citizens in 1959, the high school numbered 550 to 600 in grades ten through twelve. We had a marching band, of course, but we also had an orchestra because August Trollman taught band and orchestra in junior high and high school, and our elementary school youngsters also had started playing band and orchestra instruments. I said to myself then that I would never be a principal of a school that did not have an orchestra. And, after five schools and three decades of leading high schools, I have not, thank goodness!

The same advantage lies within STAR Theory operating schools to offer more than orchestra, such as advanced art including the graphic arts, industrial and computer technology, advanced drama, advanced music; in fact, they offer advanced courses in all of the eight areas of human knowledge and skills (science; mathematics; social studies; language arts; practical arts; fine arts; languages of other countries; and physical fitness, including health). Students in smaller school districts do not have the same opportunities, but no research has ever shown that students in such districts are less successful or less happy as adults than those who come from larger districts. And, smaller districts who adopt STAR Theory still benefit by having a larger number of students exit their schools competent or better in relevant subject matter and responsible in citizenship. Studying STAR Theory and its assumptions, one understands why this is so, assuming of course, that all conditions (assumptions) are met. Tall order? Perhaps, but well worth striving for.

When all students believe they are somebody, and that their minds are pearls, citizenship improves alongside improvement in academic pursuits. This happens when schools are smaller, and school personnel concentrate on bringing the thesis and assumptions of STAR Theory to fruition. Consider, for the moment, the chances of making such happen in school units of 400 with only 300 families to communicate with. In a STAR Theory school, steady communication between school and home to realize the school mission is a key to improved student citizenship and accomplishments in academics, but more elaboration on that comes when assumption number 9 meets the reader's eyes. The key word, then and always, is *teamwork*.

Before moving to the second part of the chapter, one more important topic is necessary: City schools!

WILL STAR THEORY WORK IN LARGE CITIES?

Small school size is even more vital to youngsters attending school in metropolitan areas, the big cities. When whites by the millions exited the large cities shortly after the middle of the twentieth century, blacks, Latinos, Asians, and other ethnicities numbered more than white youngsters among those left in the city schools. America's great cities were no longer the melting pots where ethnicities of all kinds came together. Many scribes have written about the resulting problems, so we won't go into that here. However, most of the big problems are in these cities' secondary schools, not their elementary units. Why?

Secondary schools are far too large to have organized, personalized programs to communicate often with the adults outside school who are responsible for the students who need to be inside the schools regularly to achieve in scholarship. When city secondary schools are broken into units of approximately 400 students each, school teachers and leaders have a reasonable number of families to work with. If only one of every four enrollees has a sibling in the student body of 400, only 300 families have young people enrolled in the school. Central office and school leaders mobilize forces to work with members of those families in myriad ways to exact excellence from their students in ways such as (1) increasing student attendance at least to the STAR Theory school lower limit average of 95 percent; (2) having homework phone lines between home and school for every school family to find out daily what is expected the next day and week in school; (3) meeting frequently with family members to plot strategies for assisting youngsters who are struggling; (4) setting up school unit "town meetings" at which students' family members and school personnel accent the positive in discovering ways for every youngster enrolled to become at least competent in relevant subject matter and responsible in citizenship; and (5) seeking ways to enlist everyone in the goal of knowing by heart, embracing, and treating the school mission as a living constitution. The list is just beginning in making the small secondary schools work for the students through a team effort from every stakeholder. Cities may still be giants in numbers, but STAR Theory schools are small enough to make these giants life-size, so the youngsters succeed in making prison populations smaller while graduation percentages grow larger and larger.

One thing we cannot continue in city, town, country, and suburban schools is passing youngsters to the next grade level when they have not learned to figure, read, write, and speak well enough that they are comfortable doing these things. A good synonym for comfort is *competent*. Why is it that we let the young who are still in single digits (six, seven, eight, and nine years old) move on? We are putting them is harm's way, meaning we are placing them on the track to failure. This is why in STAR Theory, we people our schools with teachers who, first, are sound in pedagogy; second, develop caring relationships with all their students; third, who reject student acts and expressions of irresponsibility; and fourth, who teach responsibility. This is why in STAR Theory schools, we have our successful pedagogues mentor those who are on their way but have not reached success. This is why in a STAR Theory school district, the most important teachers are the successful ones in elementary schools who mentor those on the road to success. We simply do not conscience any youngsters leaving elementary school without demonstrating at least competency (through the grade level they leave to attend middle or junior high) in figuring, reading, writing, and speaking. More about this in a later chapter.

In her remarkable career as a teacher and then as a principal, Deborah Meier came to the conclusion that no high school graduates more than about eighty students without lowering the quality of education youngsters take part in (Meier 1995). Reading her book, *The Power of Their Ideas*, one sees that size of school is a pivotal point in the quality of student achievement and citizenship. However, I sincerely believe that schools can graduate 100 students and still maintain the quality needed to prepare sixteen-, seventeen-, and eighteen-year-olds for life's next steps. However, in these smaller schools reside teachers responsible for guiding fewer students to subject matter competency and responsible citizenship, the word *fewer* takes us to the second part of the chapter.

CLASS SIZE AND STUDENT–TEACHER RATIO

Teaching and learning are part of the social science domain, and few researchers have shown that class size is related to student achievement until the size drops to fifteen or fewer students per teacher. Ted Sizer believes that secondary school teachers' (responsible for teaching academic subjects) optimal total load is eighty students. For those of us who have asked students to write half a dozen five-paragraph essays a quarter, or to do comparable writing assignments, eighty to a hundred seems a reasonable number for a fifty-hour work week. Pam Petitt, language arts teacher at Oak Park High School in the North Kansas City, Missouri, Schools, is an excellent source of advice about quality shortcuts in saving teacher time evaluating student essays. Pam has taught more than two and a half decades in high school, and she was despondent for quite a few years before discovering how to evaluate student papers in numbers of more than a hundred and move from the despondent mode to one of quiet exhilaration. She retires in 2001 as one of the school's best.

I have performed many demo lessons in kindergarten through grade twelve and have verified what top teachers have told me for years: When you teach the very young, such as five-, six-, seven-, eight-, and nine-year-olds, to do a quality job and remain sane enough to do it many school years, any reading, figuring, or writing lesson should have no more than fifteen children. With fifteen or fewer, a successful teacher reaches every child with the objective of each lesson. Exceed fifteen, and more than the number exceeding it, suffer academically. Put another way, if eighteen of the young described in the last paragraph are present for a lesson in the presence of a successful teacher, more than three youngsters fail to learn what the teacher wants everyone to learn in that lesson and what everyone has learned when no more than fifteen were present.

An important phrase is *no more than fifteen*. Only teachers who have taught the very young for many years know what it means to have larger classes as their responsibility. The eyes of trained, successful pedagogues do a great deal of good with kindergarten, first-, second-, and third-grade classes of twenty pupils, but they spend more time controlling a few than teaching everyone successfully. What does this mean later for the students? Some are destined to drop out of school before they graduate from high school; some are destined to fail to master reading, writing, figuring, and speaking; thus, they never achieve their potential in our free enterprise economy, and some are destined, because of dropping out and not mastering the three Rs and speaking, to face incarceration in penal institutions.

Nothing we do in this country is more vital than making our number game better for teachers in elementary schools, so the successful teachers in those classrooms can ready their young charges for learning lessons that become increasingly more difficult as they enter the next levels of learning. If we do make elementary school teachers' numbers manageable, and if we people our schools with successful teachers, another advantage is imminent: We can then teach our young to think as they learn, and as most of us know, little thinking has gone on in schools. Learning, yes; thinking, no.

CONCLUSION

Smallness in school size and class size is connected closely with student behavior. Be prepared to look at discipline in an entirely different way in the next three chapters, especially in chapter 11. The only four words that have remained unaltered in my life mission statement are the final four, ". . . be amenable to change." Everyone has surely heard, "Nothing is certain except death and taxes." As fast as the world spun in the final three-quarters of the twentieth century, the aphorism needs to read, "Nothing is certain except death, taxes, and change."

CHAPTER 10

Assumption Numbers 5 and 6

The next three assumptions lie in the area of discipline. The first deals with the most grievous—students who pose a danger to others in the school. The second is a departure from most current secondary school practice, replacing the in-school suspension area with a time-out area. These two assumptions are covered in this chapter. The third assumption in the area of discipline involves a system, and is introduced in chapter 11.

PLACE STUDENTS WHO POSE A DANGER TO OTHERS IN SCHOOL SETTINGS AWAY FROM THOSE THEY ENDANGER

Most educators and parents consider the maintenance of classroom and school discipline vital to student success in learning and thinking. I have long maintained that civilized school and classroom behavior presupposes an optimal learning and thinking environment. In STAR Theory, everyone in the school district needs assurance from the beginning of a school term that the local board of education deals firmly with extremely uncivilized student behavior—in other words, behavior that poses a danger to others. STAR Theory suggests strongly that the local board establish a written policy stating such behavior results in placing guilty students in an alternative school setting away from those they endanger or in expelling the students if an alternative school does not exist. State laws outline how this is done. For example, Missouri school principals may suspend regular students no more than ten school days at a time. The superintendent may increase this to 180 school days, and the local board of education may expand it to expulsion. If the local school district has an alternative school for extremely uncivilized student behavior, STAR Theory districts assign such students there.

Let's look at two scenarios of behavior resulting in dismissal from the school district or assignment to an alternative school. In scenario 1, Student A totes a gun to school, takes it out of his coat in the hall, points it at another student, and threatens to shoot him. A principal walking down the hall behind this action, sees and hears what is going on and disarms the student who has the gun. In the office waiting for the police to arrive, the principal hears from the student who was threatened that the student with the gun is a friend, and Student A would not have discharged the gun, that he was just kidding.

The principal who disarmed Student A says, "What you say might be the case, but our district, as you both know, has a policy that no firearms are to be at school except in the possession of a law officer. The policy says that any student who violates this policy is liable for expulsion after due process."

Student A pleads for another chance, but the principal says, "Every student has a copy of the student handbook in which the policy I have just cited is printed on page seventeen. Each homeroom teacher instructs every student to read the whole handbook and to take it home for parents to read. Additionally, every year we read this and several other board policies over the intercom three times during the first quarter and three times during the third quarter. We also discuss these with parents at Open House in the fall and in the spring. You are a junior, so you have had a handbook going on three years. As you well know, we consider possession of deadly weapons at school a serious offense. Too many tragedies have taken place in American schools; we do not want such things to happen here or anywhere else again."

A member of the local police department enters and arrests the student. The principal had called Student A's parent earlier and told her where to find her son (the police department).

Second scenario: Before school begins one morning, two students argue loudly in the hall outside the gymnasium. All of a sudden, and without physical provocation, Student C hits Student D in the nose with his fist. Student D goes down and groggily starts to get up when Student C gets on top of him and hits Student D again and again until several students pull him off Student D, who is unable to rise.

During the beating, other students have gone into the gym and yelled for a teacher to come right away. Teachers X and Z respond and come running just in time to see Student C pulled off Student D. Teacher X petitions assistance from the school nurse to attend to the injured student while Teacher Z takes IDs from eyewitnesses before escorting

Student C to the office where a principal gets the story from Teacher Z, thanks him, and sends him back to the gym. The principal calls the police department and asks for an officer to come to the school to arrest Student C.

In the ensuing conversations with Student C, Student D, and the eyewitnesses, the principal verifies the previously related incident. The police officer arrives and arrests Student C. The principal calls Student C's and Student D's parents, and relates the story as verified. Student D is conscious as the nurse administers first aid, and his parents drive him home. The principal calls the superintendent and asks for an expulsion because the district has no alternative school for such extremely uncivilized behavior. The superintendent says he will take it to the board but sees no problem if the witnesses stick with their stories.

All kinds of possibilities exist for expulsion or assignment to an alternative school within a district, but a common sense guideline to keep in mind is to ponder ahead of time what these might be, write as many as possible in publications distributed to students, periodically advertise these in myriad ways, and have the most serious ones (as with deadly weapons) written into board policy. Be certain the policy has a statement indicating the examples listed are *not* all-inclusive.

We live in different times from those in 1951 when I began teaching in a small Kansas town, and we must prepare for and stay in tune with these times. *Zero tolerance* is a relatively new term, and I believe we have gone overboard with it in many areas. However, when it comes to endangering the lives of those we are responsible for, the guilty must move elsewhere to pursue education. Take no chances! The safety of our young people, in fact, the safety of everyone who labors in a school, comes above academic and all other pursuits.

TIME-OUT ROOMS REPLACE IN-SCHOOL SUSPENSION ROOMS

More than a subtle difference exists between the words *time-out* and *suspension*. Even though *in-school* precedes *suspension*, there is a negative twist to the latter. It implies committing a transgression that keeps one away from the classroom for a predetermined length of time. It also is associated with "kicking kids out of school," something we have done for ages.

The term *time-out*, however, means taking a break from some kind of activity and place; it is a more civilized name for a place for a trans-gressing youngster to take a break from the environs where the misbe-havior occurred. *Time-out* also implies that when the youngster has had a long enough time away from the scene where the transgression was committed, the student (not an adult) decides to return with good inten-tions.

We still tend to organize, plan, and conduct school based on the mili-tary model rather than on a civilian (root word is *civil*) model. In the former, soldiers, sailors, Marines, Air Force personnel, and members of the Coast Guard prepare to protect our country with deadly force when the need arises. Schools exist, however, to prepare their residents to live civilly, that is, peacefully, capably, and responsibly in a free enterprise economy and in the world. The military model never has worked satisfactorily in schools, and it works even less satisfactorily today than it did fifty years ago. We just have not questioned strongly enough what we do the way a czarina did more than a century ago in Russia:

On a beautiful spring day she was strolling in the garden outside the palace when she observed a guard marching in a rather large circle. Curious, the czarina stopped and asked what he was guarding. He responded, "Your Highness, I have no idea. All I know is that someone succeeds me when my eight hours end each day, and someone then succeeds him. We are here around the clock."

After returning the guard to his duty, she proceeded to the library where she began investigating the reason the guards were in that palace garden twenty-four hours a day every day of the year. Eventually, she discovered that a little more than one hundred years before, a czar had a servant plant a seedling oak tree there and ordered it protected from trampling by posting guards in the area around the clock. When the czarina returned to look at the tree receiving attention even that day, it was huge, more than ten feet in diameter and scraping the sky almost a hundred feet above the ground. She immediately wrote an executive order to the palace guard commander telling him to cease guarding the royal tree. She signed, placed her royal seal on the order, and that was the end of an exercise that had continued unquestioned for more than a century.

I was not around at the beginning of the twentieth century when approximately 10 percent of American youngsters who entered grade one ultimately graduated from high school. However, it is doubtful that we needed the military model for schooling then, and few, if any, argue that one hundred years later with more than eight times that earlier number graduating from high school, we need it now. One of the remnants of the military model is suspending youngsters from school. In the next chapter, we scrutinize this problem.

When schools began implementing an in-school suspension room after 1950, the ones who originated the idea probably argued that it was a step short of an out-of-school suspension, so when they explained it to parents, it sounded more palatable. Here's how the conversation probably went:

The principal said, "Instead of suspending Ruthie from school three days, we are placing her in a new program for the same length of time. We call it our in-school suspension room. The difference is that we supervise her here in school, so you don't have to worry about what she does during the school day while you're at work. If she were suspended from school, she could not receive credit for any homework while she's gone, and you might worry about what she does all day at home alone. In our new program, however, we have a person in charge who makes certain she does her assignments in the in-school suspension room and then when she returns to class three days later she turns in the completed assignments for credit just as though she had been in class all the time."

The parent probably responded something like, "Thank goodness! Now, I'll know she's in good hands and doing her schoolwork. Thank you."

Remember, in STAR Theory, however, our goal is for every youngster to succeed in academic pursuits, and in maturing to responsible citizenship. A student is eliminated from school only for extremely uncivilized behavior like possessing deadly weapons, badly beating another human being without physical provocation or for participating in organized violence (such as a gang) in school, for turning in a false alarm, setting a fire, distributing alcohol or other drugs, and the list goes on with youngsters posing danger to others.

In a STAR Theory school districts, administrators and teachers use firm but civil consequences for student antisocial behavior. Psychologically, which in this case means cerebrally, people *behave* all the time, twenty-four hours a day for a lifetime. Human behavior has consequences. For instance, when smokers smoke over a long period, the consequence of such behavior is less physical fitness, sometimes even sickness or death. When young people read sound educational material widely and regularly over a long period, they know more things that help them socially and other ways if they use wisely what they have read. If students learn to cipher (figure) well and use these skills, they tend to be confident when dealing with others in figuring situations, and they are seldom, if ever, cheated. If we learn basic scientific principles and use them wisely, we are able to lead more efficient and effective lives. If people ingest too many calories a day and do not exercise regularly, they eventually gain weight and pay consequences for those behaviors. If someone laughs too uproariously in a church, others look and stare quizzically at the person. The list of behaviors and consequences is endless. The point is that people are always behaving, and every behavior has a consequence.

For far too long in the nation's largest social institution, school, we have reacted to uncivilized behavior with the mind-set that *punishment*, not *consequences*, leads to civil behavior.

In STAR Theory, we believe principals and teachers approach untoward student behavior firmly, but positively. Let's set a scenario to illustrate: Jack is having a tough day in school. He calls the teacher or a classmate a profane name. The teacher says, "Jack, I see you're having a tough time right now. What you just said is not a civilized word for the kind of civilized youngster you are, so I'm writing a slip for you to take down the hall to our time-out room. Please go there directly from here and present the slip to Ms. Smith. Take your books and materials with you so you'll have educational activities to work on. Cool off for a while and think through what you have just said. When you decide you are ready to settle down and calmly do your work here in class, you are welcome to return. However, give yourself a little time. We want you back, but only when you are ready to behave civilly with tongue and actions the way we both know you can."

It is important to make clear to the student what the conditions are for returning to class, but it is also important not to rub his nose in what he has done. Do it civilly and positively, the way you are asking the youngster to behave. Effective educators keep in mind that their students are clients—customers—and that they succeed with these clients only when they are successful in teaching them that the products they provide—knowledge, skills, and citizenship—are worth having, and more important, are worth having from them! This is why I stated in an earlier chapter that it is important to hold your teaching mission front and center in your mind when teaching. My mission (listen to, take seriously, affirm as significant, improve the economic well-being and quality of life of all my students) meshes perfectly with STAR Theory, but regardless of the system, I am confident you would want those nineteen words, or similar words, front and center in the minds of the teachers working with your children and grandchildren.

Let's set one more scene for ultimate time-out room referral: Two students exchange blows in the hall or on the playground. They are separated quickly before blood is spilled and escorted to the main office where the principal puts them in separate rooms to cool off a little while. She eventually talks with them separately, then together, and is satisfied that they have talked out their disagreement and are ready to return to class. First, however, she has each youngster call a parent or guardian and explain what has happened before she talks with the parent, explains what she has done and where the boys go next. The principal enters the event, their fight, in the student record software program and takes each to class.

If the principal believes more time is required to heal the rift between the boys before sending each to class, she informs the boys' parents a time-out for the remainder of the day is necessary and arranges a conference with the boys and their parents the next morning. She also asks the parents to have the boys solicit missed assignments from the school's homework telephone line that evening. The parents pick the boys up and take them home for the time-out.

At the conference in the morning, the principal determines if the boys are over their anger or if they need counseling. If the former, back to class they go; if the latter, a counselor enters the scene to take over resolution of the issue. No return to class until it is resolved. However, the school and parents (it is hoped) expect the boys to make up all work missed during time away from classes. To do otherwise is not logical.

The time-out room in the preceding case was in the main office, possibly in the counselor's office, and finally at the boys' homes. Time-out can take place almost anywhere as long as there is proper supervision. In each of the preceding scenarios, someone rejected irresponsibility and then taught responsibility. Words alone seldom, if ever, change irresponsible behavior. A few properly selected words followed by natural/logical consequences can change such behavior.

Schools exist to help students become better educated and civil people, so it is unreasonable to extend consequences that deter that mission. Even when students are expelled from a school district, the district wants them to pursue education somewhere, but not where they have endangered others. In essence, we are cutting off our noses to spite our faces if we do not truly believe this. An educated population results in a more civilized place to live.

CONCLUSION

In the next chapter, STAR Theory details a system to maintain order with firmness and kindness, not strictness or permissiveness. The system discussed in the next chapter goes hand in hand with the guidelines for meeting the assumptions of this chapter. Key concepts are doing without from within; natural and logical consequences; and respect, relevance, and reasonableness.

CHAPTER 11

Assumption Number 7

EXCEPT FOR OFFENSES THAT ENDANGER OTHERS, TEACHERS WORK WITH STUDENT TRANSGRESSIONS USING NATURAL/LOGICAL CONSEQUENCES; THUS, THEY ARE IN CHARGE OF STUDENT BEHAVIOR AND ACHIEVEMENT

Discipline plays a major part in creating exemplary student-citizens, and here is why: *Discipline is doing without from within.* It is a behavior one imposes on oneself, not on others. Successful discipline is not winning over the young through control; it is winning the young over by teaching them how to control themselves (Kahler 1999). Individuals who learn to deny significant friction and exhilaration (doing without) by transforming these invaders, with poise, into things positive (from within), are stronger by far than those who react negatively to friction and out of control to exhilaration. Those who react negatively or out of control lose significant amounts of energy, and those who transform these invasions positively and with poise increase their energy supply significantly. Verify this as I have thousands of times during my life.

Transforming friction and exhilaration positively with poise, students lay the foundation for exemplary academic achievement and citizenship. It keeps the body and mind on an even keel rather than on a bumpy road. Extreme cases of manic-depressive individuals, for instance, are either high or low much of the time because they overreact to adversity and exhilaration. More common examples are athletes who go bonkers and perform attention-getting gyrations after scoring, keeping an opponent from scoring, sacking the quarterback, or making a spectacular block or tackle where all can see the feat. They suffer great energy losses in going beyond the assignment. Because many are in excellent physical condition, the body does not suffer as much as the mind. Returning to mental focus requires time and as a result, the celebrating athlete often later makes an error costly to the team.

Professional golfers are good examples of finely tuned mental athletes who seldom lose focus because, almost immediately, they transform friction and exhilarating moments into positive poise that restores focus. Golf, by the way, is the only remaining civilized spectator sport. The golfers and most of the spectators behave as exemplary citizens for hours on end. Occasionally, their poise and attention are relieved momentarily with civilized applause.

Recall my dad's advice to me when I believed a teacher was picking on me. He said, "Danny, remember this the rest of your life: If everything were just and fair, there'd be no need for courage, so tuck in that tummy and smile!" He was telling me to do without from within; that is, do without feeling sorry for myself by transforming the sorrow I feel for myself into something positive, in this case, a smile and eventually, a good attitude. Dad, an all-American football and basketball athlete in the 1920s, is enshrined in the Kansas All Sports Hall of Fame. He played those sports and others, and later was a successful high school, college, and university coach long before it became a custom to lose oneself in friction and exhilaration following moments of denying force and great happiness. I played those sports in the 1940s; in college, I recall catching a game-clinching touchdown pass in the end zone. The custom, however, was immediately to yield control of the football to the official, which I did without fanfare before the extra point and the ensuing kickoff. Interesting how times have changed, but physical energy and mental focus continue to operate as they always have.

Smiles go a long way in changing negative feelings to positive ones. They especially do if they alter, as in my case as a young boy, self-pity into thinking about what I could do to change a teacher's actions toward me. Before long, I discovered it was my irresponsibility that caused her to correct such actions. In essence, she rejected my irresponsible acts, and my Dad taught me responsible ones to use in that situation. I was more than a little hurt at first, but Dad brought things into perspective, after which I decided to smile and listen more closely to what the teacher had to say. Why? Because Dad had developed and maintained a caring relationship with my brother and me, so we listened to him and acted on his advice.

In retrospect, I believe that had my junior high teacher first developed a caring relationship with me and her other students, and had she maintained that relationship, she would have built up enough capital in my emotional bank account (Covey 1989) that her rejection of my irresponsible acts would still have left her a balance for me to work with, without my being too upset. Of course, it would also have helped if she had taught the specific responsible behavior to overcome disappointment or hurt feelings.

History's heroes have also been those who did without from within, who transformed friction and exhilaration into something positive while maintaining their poise. Molly Pitcher did without from within day after day delivering water to soldiers on the battlefield. Abraham Lincoln went without sleep many nights waiting in the telegraph office for news of his troops in battle. In fact, most biographers said this great man got no more than four hours sleep a night for the length of time he was in office. Yet, he transformed this denying force into astute decisions. When the war was over, he transformed indescribable exhilaration into the poise of asking for a Southern favorite, *Dixie,* to be played. A civilized man was he.

Dad was an officer in the U.S. Navy on Saipan during World War II. I had just joined up and was getting ready to go to boot camp in Bainbridge, Maryland, when I received a letter from him. Here's some of what he wrote: "Remember Dan, it's emotion that makes the world go 'round, feeling, strong feeling. It's not so much what you know as it is how you feel. In fact, folks don't care how much you know until they know how much you care. . . ." He told me other important things, but these words have stuck with me the last fifty-seven years. His advice and my eventual experiences working with strong feelings through transformation have played a large part in writing this book.

In this chapter, we study how successful teachers in STAR Theory approach discipline in and out of the classroom as they set the academic stage for exemplary student achievement and citizenship.

STUDENT TARDIES AND TRUANCIES

For far too long, school administrators have taken vital tasks from teachers and in so doing, have disempowered them. Student tardiness is point one. After a certain number of student tardies, many principals want to take over, assign detentions that often lead to students not making them up, and then ultimately suspend the students. This is hardly a logical or natural consequence!

What is the natural consequence for students arriving late to class without a legitimate reason? That's easy. They are not allowed to make up what they missed before arriving. Many clever teachers begin class at least two or three times a week with a pop quiz on knowledge or skills assigned to be learned by that day. I still remember Professor Williams telling us the first day of class that critical essays counted so much toward the final grade, major exams counted so much, and pop quizzes so much. I must not have believed him because the next day he gave a pop quiz on the assignment he had announced the day before. Guess what? I had neglected to study one of the three short stories he assigned, and I paid the price. What a shock to a graduate student! Every night after that, I read and studied my assignment, all of it.

Successful teachers create and maintain a caring relationship with all students, and they realize the teacher expects them to learn and think about only subject matter relevant to living in the world they live or shall live in. These two important characteristics alone (developing and maintaining a caring relationship and expecting students to learn and think about only important stuff) get the student to school. When the successful teacher begins each class with something relevant that students are accountable for, like a pop quiz, students arrive on time. Successful teachers make every minute of class count for something valuable in the student's life now or later, and students understand why. After all, we teach youngsters only 175 to 180 days each year, and this totals less than half the calendar year. Figure that each school day is fewer than seven hours long, counting lunch, and we are talking about much less time with our students than most industrialized nations enjoy. Efficient use of teaching and learning time is vital!

When students miss something and pay a logical or natural price, the teacher rejects an irresponsible student act (not allowing them to make up an illegitimate tardy), and teaches responsibility (get here prepared, on time, and you win). When principals take this out of teachers' hands, they cripple both teachers and students.

Point two is truancies. Let's look at the typical U.S. high school. A student is truant, and so is not allowed in class until the principal writes a pass after assigning detention. Many youngsters do not show up for their detentions after or before school or at the Friday night school or in a Saturday morning study hall. Eventually, the principal suspends the truants for not making up their detentions, and what do we have?

Suspension for students who purposely skipped school. Nothing is logical or natural about this situation. In fact, it is illogical and quite unthoughtful.

What is logical and natural? Leave the truancy in the teacher's hands to write F or 0 in the grade book that day for the truant student. Further, the teacher requires the student to tell the parents what happened and to call the teacher to find how the student is faring in the course. If a parent does not call during the time designated, the teacher calls and explains everything, including the student not taking responsibility for informing the parent to call. Note, please, that the youngster is asked to take the initiative in informing the parents, an example of teaching responsibility after an irresponsible act. We don't do much of this in schools. Principals and teachers too often take responsibility away from the students by doing things themselves instead of requiring the students to do them. When youngsters perform these acts, they grow up more effectively, and they learn by doing, which makes them wiser.

This is so simple, yet we complicate things too often through unnecessary, bureaucratic actions. Teachers are adults, and they know their students better than administrators do. So, principals: Let the teachers handle their own problems, and they'll be wiser and more respected by youngsters. The same advice goes for teachers: Let students inform their parents of their own irresponsible acts. This is teaching them responsibility!

The same applies to tardies mentioned earlier. When a teacher believes a youngster has developed a habit of arriving late, the teacher simply tells the habitually tardy student to inform the parent what is happening and have the parent call the teacher. The two adults then get together with the transgressing student and plan a solution. It might be unrealistic to believe we can "heal" everyone, especially when a certain percentage of the adult population runs late fairly regularly. However, the closer to the problem people are (teachers and parents are closer to the student's problem than principals), the better the chances are for solving the problem.

In rare instances, the teacher might refer severe cases to the principal—students who are truant or tardy time after time. These referrals however, come only after the teachers have asked the school counselor to work with students who continue to experience these problems. It is unrealistic to believe these students do not exist in STAR Theory schools.

A DISCIPLINE SYSTEM

Every school requires a system for solving student behavior problems, and the system I recommend is *Positive Discipline* (Nelsen 1987). When I attended graduate school, Alfred Adler and Rudolph Dreikurs were gurus for me through their writings, so natural and logical consequence discipline has always seemed like the only sane way to work with the young, accompanied by Pygmalion Theory, of course. Johann Goethe (1963) expressed the theory more eloquently than anyone I've read: "If we take people but as they are, we make them worse; if we treat them as though they were what they should be, we bring them whither they should be brought." My parents reared my brother and me with that in mind.

Long ago, I eliminated the word *punishment* from my usable vocabulary. Jane Nelsen wrote another book, *Positive Discipline in the Classroom* (1989), but I recommend the first one because it is useful to teachers and parents, and STAR Theory is a team affair. Without the schools, the parents, and the community joining to improve student achievement and citizenship, no system improves what we do.

To teach well and to implement positive discipline effectively, one must have an understanding of the various needs human beings possess inherently. It is inherent to survive, to love and to be loved, to feel important, to experience a normal degree of freedom, and to enjoy living. For a more complete understanding of these genetic needs, read *Choice Theory* (Glasser 1998). To save time, you might wish instead to read chapters 4, 5, and 6 of *The Quality School* (Glasser 1992). Note that in this work, Glasser called it *Control Theory,* which he later changed to the more palatable *Choice Theory.*

Successful teachers use the three Rs when working with students. They treat them with *respect*, and issue consequences that are *relevant* and *reasonable* (Nelsen 1987). At first, this seems like a given, but most of us have experienced teachers, bosses, and even parents, who have dispensed unreasonable and irrelevant consequences disrespectfully. This is no way to win friends and influence people. A wonderful, student-empowering way to implement consequences is through class meetings (Nelsen 1987).

Many primary grade teachers use class meetings every school day. Intermediate grade pedagogues often believe by the time the youngsters are conditioned the first few years of school to class meetings, their need lessens in grades four and five, so they conduct these meetings only two or three times a week. Because students might come to middle and high schools from schools that do not have class meetings or do not use the three Rs of discipline, teachers start over in explaining the reasons for them and then schedule these meetings once a week or as needed.

Here's how class meetings work: Prepare students well before the first one. Tell them that when they have problems to resolve, rather than take them into their own hands, they should write each one on a piece of paper and place the paper in a special box or jar on your desk. If they change their minds before the class meeting, they can remove their paper from the box. Delaying discussion of problems allows the heat of the moment to pass before discussion begins. Many problems can be resolved without bringing them up in the meeting.

When setting up the meeting, place the chairs or desks in a circle so everyone sees everyone else's face, not the nape of the neck. The teacher asks each person to think of a compliment for another person in the room. Ask each to be specific, not general, when complimenting the person. If the student cannot think of a specific compliment, tell the student to say, "I pass." By starting with compliments, the setting is calm before students discuss problems. Also, explain that when the teacher reads each problem placed in the box or jar, the student who placed it there follows by saying something like, "I put that one there, and here's my suggested solution."

It is important for the teacher to set the ground rules before students discuss problem resolution: Everyone talks respectfully to and about others even if someone has been unkind. Suggestions for consequences must be reasonable and related to the perceived transgressions. Before beginning the first class meeting, the teacher presents scenarios with reasonable and relevant solutions. On occasion, especially at first, the teacher enters discussions and points out students' suggestions that are not reasonable and relevant (Nelsen 1987). Above all, the teacher maintains an atmosphere of respect during class meetings as she does during the entire school day.

Another excellent book for preparing teachers for class meetings and logical/natural consequence discipline is Glasser's *The Quality School Teacher* (1993). Chapter 11 of this book is especially relevant to teaching students Choice Theory in a class meeting setting. Before reading it, however, read either chapters 4, 5, and 6 in *The Quality School* (1992) or the book *Choice Theory* (1998).

A MOST IMPORTANT CHANGE

Here is assumption number 7: Except for offenses that endanger others, teachers work with all student transgressions using natural or logical consequences. Teachers do not refer them to principals or headmasters to assign consequences; thus, teachers are in charge of student behavior and achievement.

Some schools in the United States might follow this assertion, but if so, I do not know where they are. However, this assumption makes perfectly good sense. The best teachers, the most outstanding local, state, national, and international leaders, the most effective workers, and the best parents live with a sense of control and direction. They are confident human beings who take exemplary initiatives. They handle their own problems to the best of their abilities, and their abilities are myriad. Let's look at teachers as examples.

Teachers who make a habit of sending misbehaving students to the office are simply looking for trouble and probably lose total control of their students eventually. Students have always responded well to teachers who manage their own classrooms well. Even habitually mis-behaving youngsters look up to teachers who are in control and who handle their own problems, and they often improve their behavior with such teachers (Swick 1980).

Successful teachers refer students to principals only when they are mandated to do so. For example, if a student is obviously under the influence of something that causes erratic behavior (such as alcohol or other drugs), the teacher needs to have the principal come to the class-room to take charge of that youngster so she can continue her teaching responsibilities. If students begin fighting physically in the classroom, she takes the same action.

However, most insubordinate acts and expressions, and other uncivil student behavior that does not require office intervention result in the teacher simply and calmly saying something like, "It's obvious you are having difficulty transforming (a familiar word in a STAR Theory school) your negativity (or hyperactivity) into acceptable learning behavior right now, Samuel. I'm writing you a pass to go to our time-out room, where you can get away from whatever is causing this. Please take all your books and belongings and report to the time-out room directly from here. If I don't see you the rest of the period, I'll know you are there, and I'll call tonight at home so we may discuss whether you believe you are ready to return to class tomorrow. Make certain, however, you have discussed this with a parent so after you and I talk, I can talk with your parent." (In the last sentence, the teacher follows up with a parent only in more serious situations, so the teacher protects herself and has it on record in the student's file in case something happens in the future. Otherwise, the student returns to class when he is ready to behave normally. In the meantime, he is expected to keep up with his class work.)

There are exceptions to everything, of course. Earlier, I mentioned teachers sending students to the office for situations that interfere with their teaching other students, like fighting or appearing to be under the influence of alcohol, other drugs, or something indiscernible. The principal decides whether the behavior was a danger to others or just to the student under the influence or fighting. Some cases result in expulsion or sending the student to an alternative school. If the behavior is not serious enough to warrant alternative school or expulsion, the principal in a STAR Theory school does everything possible to return the student to class as early as feasible because exemplary student achievement and citizenship are the school's most important products.

Let's take fighting, for example. If the combatants work the situation out amicably, the logical consequence for a fight could be researching the tragic results of fights from the past and reporting the results to a class, or writing a paper that the teacher reads to the class in which the fight happened, or to the classes assembled at that time in the hall where it happened. Logical and natural consequences abound for almost every untoward behavior, consequences that are far superior to student expulsion or transfer (when the student fighters agree to be peaceful, that is). When combatants cannot agree to peace between themselves, a cooling off period at home might be the only logical consequence. Counselors also definitely are brought into peace negotiations.

CONCLUSION

Some readers might believe that it is impossible to change enough homes, families, guardians, or children to realize the thesis assertions in this book. These doubters might say that STAR Theory is a pipe dream that will never come to fruition. Evil does exist in the world. In human beings, evil is the absence of empathy and of positive regard for human beings who do not share the evil one's habits or beliefs. Empathy, as I described earlier, is the ability to feel as others feel, and when one adds this characteristic to positive regard for fellow humans, one diminishes evil or latent evil. Successful teachers not only possess these two characteristics, they also are genuine people, not phonies who speak with forked tongues. For this reason, it is essential that each school in a STAR Theory district fortify itself with as many successful teachers as possible and as soon as they can. When school districts have at least half a staff of successful teachers, these noble and valuable human beings make significant inroads into eliminating evil. That is worthy of striving to achieve, and not worthy of giving up!

The preceding might sound a little like a Stephen King novel, but good has overcome evil for centuries, and there is no reason for this to change. This then is why *positive discipline* is so important in schools, especially in a STAR Theory school. Perhaps now, it is easier to understand one of the greatest minds ever to inhabit a physical body, Johann Goethe, when one reads again his magnificent aphorism. With logical/ natural consequence discipline administered respectfully, relevantly, and reasonably by successful, genuine teachers who have high empathy and unconditional positive regard for all their students, Goethe's assertion makes perfect sense: *"If we take people but as they are, we make them worse; if we treat them as though they were what they should be, we bring them whither they should be brought."*

Continue reading. The battle for exemplary schools that produce *more* exemplary Americans is just warming to the task!

CHAPTER 12

Assumption Numbers 8 and 9

This chapter continues with the theme of building ownership in the creation of district and school missions that support STAR Theory. After stakeholders create the missions that support STAR Theory, constant attention to the involvement of stakeholders is paramount, for without involvement, it is unlikely that the required support is resident. Although it is true that we value most what we contribute to and value least what we are not part of, if we do not continue to be part of something, we eventually lose interest.

TEACHERS, ADMINISTRATORS, AND BOARD MEMBERS SUPPORT STAR THEORY

One can accurately say that in a flourishing organization, employees support the system the organization uses, and the organization is based on a vision and a mission. However, not everyone works with a system that directly affects the young. Why many teachers, administrators, and board members fail to develop and organize a network to work closely with one another has puzzled me for a long time. Largeness gets in the way of many, I suppose, but there is no reason small districts cannot organize for elucidation and cooperation between and among teachers, administrators, and board members.

In districts implementing STAR Theory, it is essential for these groups to understand their district and school missions, to implement and support them, and even to revise them. For that reason, an ongoing inservice program is in place in STAR Theory schools.

Who Is in Charge of the Inservice Program?

Each school principal is the logical choice for running the inservice program, and it is hoped that the principal has a thorough understanding of the ramifications of STAR Theory. As W. Edwards Deming wrote in his seminal book, *Out of the Crisis* (1986), and I paraphrase, those who manage people need to be able to perform well the tasks their followers perform daily. Of Deming's fourteen points, this one and constancy of purpose are the most important in the schooling of young people. Exemplary principals have been and still are successful teachers, so they understand and know how to teach STAR Theory to other adults in and out of the school. How this happens is up to the principal and the staff in each school, but keep in mind that unless teachers, administrators, and board members understand the implications of STAR Theory and the district mission, it is difficult to support either.

The most natural place for board members to learn about STAR Theory is in the schools their youngsters attend. Board members who have no children in school can learn about it in a school in their area. Administrators (other than principals) and other central office leaders also learn about the system in an orientation program a principal conducts in the school.

Let us say that one board member and four central office leaders live in the Utopia Elementary School attendance area. Utopia Principal Jane Jones receives this information from the district personnel director and contacts the board member and central office leaders who reside in the Utopia Elementary School attendance area, inviting them to an introductory meeting designed to set up a schedule of STAR Theory orientation meetings at the school. Utopia Elementary School Principal Jones contacts the superintendent, of course, before she does any of the groundwork previously explained. It is hoped that the superintendent has already informed central office administrators and board members what is about to take place.

A Board of Education STAR Theory orientation program is an excellent way to start the ball rolling. In this meeting, the superintendent talks with the board, ideally in concert with an eloquent district principal about what each principal is going to be doing in the near future; that is, the principals contact board members and central office administrators who live in the principals' attendance areas to attend a series of STAR Theory meetings. The purpose of the meetings in the school settings is to orient board members and central office administrators about the thesis and assumptions of STAR Theory. Later, when central office members teach in these schools periodically (explained in chapter 7), each understands the intricacies of the system. Also, board members who are free once in a while might want to take a shot at using STAR Theory by pinch-hitting in a classroom. Many board members have at one time been teachers, and, it is hoped, good ones.

What individual principals do in their STAR Theory orientation sessions with central office leaders and board members, and how many sessions they conduct are up to them, but it is imperative for each school leader to practice STAR Theory in every session. The reason is obvious. No central office administrator, other leader, or board member should begin pinch-hitting for school teachers until these orientation sessions are successfully concluded, and they have witnessed models conducting the orientation sessions. School principals might wish to consider some kind of certificate for each central office leader and board member completing the sessions successfully. This is a classy final touch that helps cement support of the system. Here's another suggestion for principals: Include exemplary and articulate successful teachers in conducting the orientation sessions. The more participants who experience such teachers demonstrating STAR Theory, the more the participants see teachers and the system in a good light. This is another way to facilitate support of the district's decision to enhance students' success. When teachers help in these meetings, the principal is present, of course, and successful teachers who team with the principal need substitutes during the sessions they are helping facilitate. This brings up another important point: substitute teachers and STAR Theory.

Substitute teachers also need orientation, so they promote, rather than detract from, STAR Theory. Substitutes have a tough enough job when they take over for an absent teacher. Ideally, the district has enough funds to purchase copies of this book for aspiring district substitutes to read before attending an orientation session that most districts conduct before the school year. In addition to the usual items on the agenda at such a meeting, an elementary, middle, and high school principal are present to discuss STAR Theory and answer questions substitutes have about the book before venturing into a district school to teach. Teaching well is not an easy task. The orientation session leaders spend extra time explaining in detail what the district and various school missions mean to every teacher who engages the young. They go into detail also about pedagogy, rejecting student acts and expressions of irresponsibility, and they provide examples of how to teach students responsibility. They make certain the substitutes understand the concept of the time-out room. Nothing is left to chance in employing capable substitute teachers who are willing to learn about and implement STAR Theory, just as nothing is left to chance in employing teachers. Some substitutes drive from their homes in other districts to perform their duties. Some come from backgrounds of strictness or permissiveness. In STAR Theory schools, they change these old-fashioned, ineffective habits into using firmness with dignity and respect, and freedom with order. Students have limited choices (firmness), and students make choices that show respect for everyone, including themselves. As I wrote in the November 1999 *Bulletin*, to be successful in discipline, one does not win over the young by controlling them; one wins the young over by teaching them how to control themselves (doing without from within). That's simply sound common sense. A teacher who does this teaches students responsibility, a key skill for succeeding anywhere, anytime.

When teachers (including substitutes), administrators, and board members understand STAR Theory, they are bound to support it because every facet represents student competence or better in relevant knowledge and skills, and responsibility in citizenship. This takes us to assumption number 9.

ADULTS WORKING WITH STUDENTS TREAT THE DISTRICT AND THEIR OWN SCHOOLS' MISSIONS AS CONSTITUTIONS

The district mission is a living document; that is, it is present in the lives of everyone connected with the schools every moment during the school day and when preparing for the school day in the minds and actions of those who facilitate the positive growth of relevant student knowledge, skills, and citizenship. Those who facilitate such things include all who work in the district. I spent considerable time in an early chapter discussing the importance for every teacher to possess a vision and a teaching mission. The teachers' visions and missions are compatible with the district mission, which is a living constitution. Teachers live by the district mission every moment in their jobs. It should be short enough (no longer than twenty-five words) for everyone to call front and center in the mind before making important decisions. Let's create one for a moment and discuss how associates (employees) use it. Keep in mind that its creation at the district level comes from the input of many sources (people who live in, work in, and attend school in the district). The following is an example of an inclusive, yet briefly stated, mission in an imaginary school district: *The Highroad Schools strive to improve the economic well-being and quality of life of all their students.* With that concise statement (seventeen words), it is easy to place front and center in an associate's mind any moment an important decision is considered. For instance, if I place my own teaching mission under it, is it compatible with Highroad's? Remember mine from an earlier chapter? *Listen to, take seriously, affirm as significant, improve the economic well-being and quality of life of all my students.* Nineteen words there that fit nicely with the Highroad Schools' mission, would you agree? In fact, I'd say that each school in the Highroad district might wish to consider the mission as its own. Improve it if you can, but remember to keep it brief and all inclusive so you can retrieve it to the front and center of your mind when needed. That's really important, or why create missions?

If you believe it is not specific enough, consider this: The curriculum within each school classroom and the success with which it (the curriculum) becomes part of each student's mind and being contain the specifics that make the mission a reality or a bust. Detailed school curriculum is for another book. How people within a district help make the curriculum part of each youngster before each exits is the subject of this book. That is one of the book's most important assertions, so let's state it another way for emphasis: If the teachers create teaching missions that support the district and school missions, and they are successful in producing students who leave school at least competent in relevant subject matter and responsible in citizenship, they have done their parts in exemplary fashion. Do you see now why successful teachers are the STARs of every school, and why their associates labor to help them shine more brightly? It is so simple, yet we often lose ourselves by complicating things so much. Again, successful teachers are the STARs! Others work diligently to support their efforts.

I shall say it again with more specifics: All others who work with/ for students (food service personnel, custodians, nurses, secretaries, principals, bus drivers, substitute teachers, instruction assistants, superintendents, directors, and others) obligate themselves, when signing on board, to support the STARs (successful teachers) and the district/ school missions in their every word and action to improve the economic well-being and quality of life of every Highroad district student, assuming that is the district mission created and agreed to by those with vested interests in student success.

Who Inservices Those Who Do Not Teach?

Those who do not teach students contractually have leaders who are the logical ones to teach their people the intricacies of the thesis and assumptions of STAR Theory. Examples: The leader in charge of custodians teaches the custodians. The leaders of the various secretaries teach them; each school principal teaches the secretaries in the school, the superintendent teaches the superintendent's secretaries, and the head of nurses teaches the nurses. Each category of personnel has a leader, and that leader teaches those within the category.

An earlier chapter covered school and central office leaders practicing STAR Theory; thus, every department has a leader who understands STAR Theory. Do not underestimate the value of teaching STAR Theory to those who do not teach or lead. These vital people go home each evening; they have friends and families; they talk with hundreds of folks, and some of the talk is about the school district in which they labor. Be certain, through exemplary teaching, that these individuals understand what the district is doing each day with students!

Furthermore, all associates (employees) in the Highroad Schools evaluate themselves on the success of their daily jobs and on implementing the district mission (and school mission if that associate works in a school). This is why it is important for all associates to understand STAR Theory and the specific import of the district and school missions.

I'll go further, even those associates in districts who exist under a system other than STAR Theory are obligated the same way. When we put it all together, including the next chapter, it is easy to understand why most school systems in the United States and throughout the world are not working in the best interests of all students: Those vested do not work together. It's like the young, freckle-faced Danny Kahler who believed the man who told him to rub his face in the morning dew on grass at dawn on that long ago May day in 1936, because if he did, his freckles would turn into a coat of tan! Danny did what the elderly man told him to do, but it turned out to be a joke. More than superstition is necessary to cause things to happen in life and in schools.

CONCLUSION

Developing successful teachers in small schools with reasonably sized groups of youngsters who pose no danger to anyone, who are supported by those who work with them and by the parents of their students, we still have another "necessary" to meet. This book is written to change schools in a nation that began with a 1776 Declaration of Independence, an instrument written by a genius to change things significantly with a new nation. The declaration's author, Thomas Jefferson, also knew the importance of an informed citizenry. He knew that if the vast majority of that citizenry does not stay knowledgeable about the nation, the citizenry receives what it deserves, less than the best. Chapter 13 is vital for the success of something else Jefferson believed in—the education of all our citizens, not just the privileged few. Involvement of all community adults is the key!

Assumption Number 10

TWO-THIRDS OR MORE OF THE COMMUNITY STAKEHOLDERS TREAT THE DISTRICT AND THEIR RESPECTIVE SCHOOL MISSIONS AS CONSTITUTIONS

"Aye, there's the rub," Shakespeare knowingly scribed when a predicament loomed on the horizon. The title of this chapter predicts battles unless certain conditions are present. One condition, and perhaps the most important, is having small school units, which means small attendance area populations that lend easily to communication between school personnel and the citizens who live in the attendance areas. Not everyone who lives in a school attendance area has children who attend school; however, if 350 youngsters attend Utopia Elementary School, it is essential that adults (with and without children) who live in the Utopia attendance area know the school and district missions. That is one important reason missions are concise, such as, "With community support in attracting and keeping successful teachers, the Highroad Schools strive to improve the quality of life of all students." Utopia Elementary School is wise in stating, "We are part of the Highroad Schools and as team players, our mission is the district mission, word for word."

We are now drawing closer to the secret of producing students who are at least competent in relevant subject matter and responsible in citizenship. The secret, of course, is in everyone pulling together to produce competent, quality, and responsible graduates of the Highroad Schools. The mission statement then, is much better than the seventeen-word mission viewed in the last chapter because this one includes another condition—community support in attracting and keeping successful teachers. Without that in the mission, people expect miracles from educators alone, and such miracles do not happen. A village helps rear children, and a village helps educate those same children. Attracting and keeping successful teachers implies much, including sensible numbers of youngsters per teacher and salaries that keep successful teachers in the Highroad Schools. The one thing a district cannot afford is to lose successful teachers. Everyone in the village (city, suburb, town, and hamlet) is acutely aware of the responsibility of producing successful graduates of the Highroad Schools, and one reason is community involvement in and the schools' distribution of an important document.

Schools need a document its residents believe in, and because human beings value most what they contribute to, and value least what they are not part of, school leaders involve all segments of the community in creating such documents. How they go about doing this is a local decision, but if such documents do not exist, there is no way for the majority of the community to understand completely what the schools believe in and what goes on in their schools. P. C. Schlechty (1990) wrote in his book, *Schools for the 21st Century*, that each school district needs a "we believe" statement. A STAR Theory district involves a cross-section of its community in producing a document similar to the one Schlechty wrote in his visionary book. The eventual manifesto created by the citizens of the district is promoted in such ways that the statement becomes operational throughout the district. Every eligible voting resident in the Highroad Schools has a copy of such a document created by the district stakeholders. The following is a suggestion for that document. However, it is important to involve district stakeholders in creating the document each district decides it needs. Otherwise, if not enough citizens from across the school district take part, community buy-in does not happen.

THE HIGHROAD SCHOOLS MANIFESTO

Mission: With community support in attracting and keeping successful teachers, the Highroad Schools strive to improve the quality of life of all students.

1. Afforded the right opportunities, every youngster learns the necessaries (an old-fashioned word, and a good one). School professionals

create opportunities every day for each youngster to learn the neces-saries.

The key: It is essential for teachers to be certain that every student is "on board" before they teach the necessaries. Elementary? It is not! Every day in virtually every school in this country many youngsters simply fail to understand the importance of the opportunities (relevant knowledge and skills) awaiting them. The best way to bring everyone on board is to involve each in providing reasons for learning the neces-saries. (The example that follows is not part of the manifesto, but is included for readers to understand the rationale behind the assertions. The same applies to other examples in the points that follow)

Example: A teacher asked me in February about twenty years ago if he could attend an upcoming social studies conference. I said, "Go and learn; I'll sub for you on one condition: I teach my own lesson plan." He agreed, and off he went.

I'll provide the scenario in one of his classes, a remedial social stud-ies group. I taught all students the value of knowing where they were in relation to the world immediately around them. Now, if I had pon-tificated the reasons for knowing the states immediately surrounding Missouri, students would soon have forgotten why this was valuable knowledge. However, I gave each coming into the room at the begin-ning of the period a map without the names of the states, but with the outlines of Missouri and the eight states immediately surrounding and touching it.

I took roll, announced the lesson plan, and said that our mother had told my brother and me when we were young that her native state, Mis-souri, was one of the two most popular states in the nation. We asked why, and she said that only two states had as many as eight states touching them, Missouri and Tennessee, and that Tennessee touched her state, Missouri.

We then had a discussion about why it was important to know the states surrounding ours. I continued by telling the students I was not going to share those reasons with them because it's bad teaching to do so. Instead, I asked them to tell me why it is important to know where each of those eight is located around Missouri. I got them started by giving one reason: Watch the television weather man discuss an approaching storm and point to a map that does not have the names of the states, just their geographic shapes. I told them I knew where the storm was coming from, for instance, and where it was going even though the states were not labeled on his television weather map. From that point, the class rattled off at least a dozen or so reasons it was important to know which state was which in relation to Missouri. Next, I placed them in learning teams with a mission: Come up with an acronym (I explained the word) that makes it easy to remember the states that touch Missouri.

First, however, I related that Mother had taught my brother and me the whole world in similar ways. I used Central America as an example. Mother told us to *beg* her to tell us the first three countries. We begged, and she said, **B**eliz, **E**l Salvador, **G**uatemala. Then she said to remember **H**ow **N**ice **C**hildren **P**lay—**H**onduras, **N**icaragua, **C**osta Rica, **P**anama.

To make certain they knew I was not pulling their legs, I described how she taught us the ten provinces of Canada: From West to East, **BASMOQ**, three **N**'s and a **PE** (**B**ritish Columbia, **A**lberta, **S**askatchewan, **M**anitoba, **O**ntario, **Q**uebec, then the three **N**'s are **N**ewfoundland. **N**ova Scotia, **N**ew Brunswick, and the **PE** is **P**rince **E**dward Island). She said we'd just have to memorize the Yukon and Northwest Territories, which are not provinces. As I was relating the past, for credibility, I used maps to point out the countries and provinces, but I turned away to show that I still knew them. Additionally, I mentioned that any time I read about a country in the newspaper, see one on television, or hear it mentioned in a conversation, I have an immediate picture of that country in my mind's eye. Then, they went to work in learning teams.

Before long, a member of one team hollered, "D. K., we've got it!"

I said, "All right, shoot."

Excitedly, another member of the team sounded off, "IN COAT."

Someone on another team sarcastically piped up, "I can understand IN stands for Iowa and Nebraska, and OAT is Oklahoma, Arkansas, and Tennessee, but Kansas starts with a K, not a C, guys!"

Then, a third member of the IN COAT originators shot back, "Yeah, you're right, Josh, but we thought it was kinda clever because everywhere you go, intentionally misspelled signs pop out to wake you up and get your attention. So you see, when we came up with IN COAT, we thought it was a good idea even though Kansas starts with a K, not a C." (Out of the mouths of babes!)

I intervened and exclaimed, "Great idea, team; we'll use it." How about the last two states, Kentucky and Illinois?

"Ain't got there yet," came the answer, so I put the teams back to work, and in just a few minutes, another team's members waved their hands as though they had discovered people on Mars.

"We have it, D.K. IN COAT KAHLER IDIOT!"

Removing my coat slowly and placing it on the desk, I asked, "What was that you said?"

Joel, from the team that offered IN COAT KAHLER IDIOT, came back with, "Can't say it with your coat off, D.K.!"

So, I slowly and calmly put my coat back on, and when the second arm went through the second sleeve, and my coat was on again, virtually the whole class shouted, "IN COAT KAHLER IDIOT!"

I smiled and said, "That's probably one of the cleverest and most creative acronyms I have ever heard. Let's go with it!" (They applauded and laughed.)

Then, I said, "We'll go over this with the maps I gave you, and you write the names of the states where the names belong except for Missouri. Across Missouri, write IN COAT KAHLER IDIOT. Next week, the first time you see me anywhere in school, come up and say the magic acronym, IN COAT KAHLER IDIOT, then tell me what each letter stands for, and I'll give you a free pen or a free lunch, your choice."

In the time we had remaining, we went over the states surrounding Missouri, and everyone seemed to have them down pat. I even tossed in the capital cities and told them if they could identify those (not really important, though, just fun), I'd give them both pen and lunch. They wrote the capital cities' names on the respective states on the map I gave each.

The following week (the classes I taught were on a Friday), every student came up to me at one time or another and correctly identified the states surrounding Missouri via IN COAT KAHLER IDIOT. One of them caught me in the cafeteria and yelled from the back the magic words.

I looked around and asked, "Where are you, my friend?"

He responded, and I tossed him a pen, which he caught.

You might be wondering about the last episode, whether it was showing disrespect in front of several hundred other students in the cafeteria. The answer is a resounding, "No!" Everyone knew I did strange things to elicit answers so that I could give students free pens or lunches. Before graduating, probably half the students earned one or the other or both, at least once.

Oh, about the capitals, quite a few took the time to learn these so they could collect both prizes. As I said, however, capital cities are not instructive to know for most youngsters, and I spent little time teaching these.

Postscript: I asked the teacher to let me come back and assess my students the next Friday, and everyone remembered all eight states that bordered Missouri, and in the right order. I also asked if I could do it again once in April and once in May. Same results. Every time I returned to his class, no student failed to get every state right. Many remembered capitals, too. I still see some of these students, now adults, in various parts of Greater Kansas City, and they often remind me that they still know the eight states via IN COAT KAHLER IDIOT! I always take time to ask why it's important, and not once has anyone failed to give me a good answer.

The point was that getting every youngster "on board" at the beginning of a valuable lesson is a pivotal step in becoming a successful teacher. Once a teacher has every student on board, pedagogy continues, and successful teachers are, after all, outstanding in pedagogy! As pedagogues, some probably guessed why I took my coat off slowly and then did the same putting it back on. Right. It was to create memory in my students, and creating memory by using business like that is an excellent way to help students retain what the teacher wants them to learn. Any time a teacher surrounds students with warmth during secondary reinforcement, learning sticks (unless what one has learned goes unused long enough, of course).

2. What we teach students helps determine their opportunities. School leaders (principals and teachers) furnish schoolwork that yields success in school and leads to success in students' later lives.

Example: Often, some youngsters stumble when learning long division and as a result, have problems with that portion of numbers later in school and certainly, later in the adult world. If a student has learned to add, subtract, multiply, and use short division correctly, teachers must make certain that no student stumbles in long division. The simple pedagogical aid of Dad (divide), Mom (multiply), Sister (subtract), Brother (bring down next number) has brought order and help to countless students who have had trouble with long division because they could not remember what to do next. The methods teachers use in presenting information are crucial, but the information teachers provide is just as crucial. So, be certain everyone is on board when setting the stage, then keep them on board and on balance in presenting the relevant information.

3. Schools are knowledge/thinking/skill institutions with students as the receivers of opportunities to work with knowledge/thinking/skill-related products.

Example: The Information Age or dot.com world we live in! Among tools from years of yore (such as textbooks, library books, notebook paper, and pens), the school also makes available to students the electronic world of computers and fits it into the various courses of studies. The young go home and to jobs that have computers; thus, the schools make computers a normal part of the school learning environment. The time might not be far off when students write papers in classrooms on software housed in laptop computers, print the papers on classroom printers, and turn them in before leaving class. How much easier to read student writing productions this will be!

4. Teachers are leaders just as executives are; principals are leaders of teachers or leaders of leaders. Curriculum is the raw material for student use, and leaders organize the system of schooling to yield the greatest likelihood for students' successful engagement with knowledge/thinking/skills. This is called providing the right stuff with the right lures and it goes back to setting the stage properly so that every student is on board. That is why it takes time to find the right lure for each student. Teachers cannot know everything, so the successful ones entice the students to furnish reasons for learning the stuff so it becomes the right stuff for each youngster. Often, the clever teacher has a popular student, motivated and multidimensional in interests, lead the students aboard by offering several lures. Young people, after all, are more knowledgeable of their peers' culture than adults are. Or as I wrote in an earlier chapter, adults and youngsters today have different values and cultures.

5. The superintendent's primary role is to educate the community about the mission of the schools, to promote community participation in the realization of that mission, and to ensure that results dominate everyone's attention. District leaders accomplish these things by using the strengths and talents of the board of education, the other leaders in the central office and the schools, and by making themselves regularly visible in the community. The superintendent is pivotal in community knowledge of the Highroad Schools manifesto and in community adoption and treatment of district and school missions as constitutions.

6. Teachers and principals are accountable for results once STAR Theory is in place. Expected results: All students do relevant schoolwork in which they experience success and from which they gain

socially and culturally valued knowledge/thinking/skills (relevant subject matter competency and responsible citizenship).

7. Obligation of the superintendent, the board of education, and the members of the community: They provide students, teachers, and principals those conditions and forms of support to ensure optimal performance, continuing growth, and development. To accomplish this, each school is open every school day and during many evening activities to all members of the community, and community members know it! Senior citizens, especially, are welcome through numerous avenues and are always admitted free to events sponsored solely by the schools. A school volunteer program, like Youth Friends, is in force, and successful interaction between the schools and the community means thousands of community-member hours are spent in the various Highroad Schools each year.

8. The Highroad Schools ensure working conditions that equate with the professional status of all associates employed here, and confirm the importance of tasks assigned to these professionals. The Highroad Schools management team and board of education treat associates with respect in public and in private.

9. Continuing improvement, thoughtful, persistent innovation, and commitment to continuing growth are expectations of all people and programs supported by district resources, and district resources must be committed to ensure that associates and programs meet these expectations.

10. Requirement for all students to succeed: A sound, continuing, and organized program to place the Highroad Schools manifesto's beliefs in the minds and actions of at least two-thirds, if not all, of the district's voting population. Purpose: Convince district citizens to treat the district and their respective school missions as constitutions. This enhances the students' chances to succeed.

With the manifesto and its requisite action, the final condition, assumption number 10, is in place, and STAR Theory is ready to roll into production of competent, quality, and responsible graduates.

CONCLUSION

The next chapter puts things in perspective for readers who believe that successful American schools are possible throughout the land, no matter where they are located. The major ingredients are a preponderance of STARS in each school—successful teachers; small schools and decent numbers of students in the classrooms that allow people to communicate effectively; visionary leadership throughout the schools; and an unquenchable desire by stakeholders to make all youngsters successful!

CHAPTER 14

The STARs

The theater is almost full. Ushers are seating the last comers swiftly, with a flourish of welcome, and counting the minutes until curtain time. The audience settles, looks around, reads the program to find out where act 1 takes place, and then the lights begin to dim. You almost feel, more than hear, a kind of sigh of contentment, anticipation. Playgoers in the back lean forward; a hand in the darkness seeks and finds another to say, "Now it's beginning, this is what we wanted." Down front they lean back ready and happy. It's dark. Slowly, the curtain parts, and another world opens in brightness and surprise. This is . . . the school classroom of a STAR! Every school day literally thousands of young students can hardly wait to enter a STAR's classroom, where they converse, collaborate, think, and wonder. They experience joy, delight, achievement, and relief; and learn—and depart too soon, they realize. Ultimately, however, these fortunate youngsters put the conversations, the collaborations, the thinking, the wonder, the joy, delight, achievement, relief, and the learning into their worlds outside those STARs' classrooms, and that equates with schooling the way it is supposed to be.

The bottom line of this book is finding and developing a plethora of STARs to people the nation's classrooms so virtually every student who enters school exits at least competent in relevant subject matter and responsible in citizenship. STARs are not only outstanding in pedagogy, they create caring relationships with all their students. STARs reject student acts and expressions of irresponsibility and then teach responsibility without diminishing previously established caring relationships with their students because they always have enough in their students' emotional bank accounts (Covey 1989).

Again, every STAR Theory school has at least a majority of STARs resident, or it is moving in that direction. Additionally, when STARs are absent for whatever reason, knowledgeable and effective substitutes who embrace STAR Theory pinch-hit for them. Others who labor in the schoolhouse and in the various district edifices and places support the STARs in quality ways so that they shine more brightly. Why? So all students have optimal opportunities to learn, to think, and to acquire skills to enhance the quality of their lives as responsible citizens in school and forever more. None of this happens, however, without the support of the community in attracting and in keeping successful teachers, the STARs. Attracting successful teachers is one thing, but keeping them is quite another. Keeping them involves community commitment to create and maintain small schools and small classes, and to remunerate successful pedagogues enough to make them content and happy to be where they are, doing what they do. Seldom do STARs wish to lead schools or districts because they love what they do and are compensated justly for doing it. Occasionally, however, a STAR sees the need to lead outside the classroom, and that is why school and district leaders are former STARs—successful teachers.

Specifically, what does a community receive for such support and commitment? Here are some of the perks for a community willing to do these things for their young people:

1. Teachers handle their own problems using positive discipline. Exception: Students who pose a danger to others are placed in alternative environs.
2. Youngsters learn to handle their own problems in responsible, positive ways because successful teachers teach that kind of responsibility. Therefore, student achievement and attendance rise, and student antisocial behavior diminishes.
3. Emphasis in the school district is on every student achieving at least competence in relevant subject matter; however, without teaching students responsibility, teachers deprive the young of the ability to deliver the *Message to Garcia*. If this story is missing from the reader's past, let it be no more, at least in short, so the reader later searches for the whole story in a huge library over whose portal (it is hoped) hangs James Lowell's great question and response, which I paraphrase: Have you ever considered what the ability to read means? It is the key that admits one to the company of the saint and the sage, of the wise and the witty, at their wisest and wittiest moments. But now, on to one of the greatest stories of the nineteenth century.

The impact of Hubbard's (1899) tale throughout the world was amazing. Members of the U.S. Marine Corps and eventually, Boy Scouts received a copy. Russian railway workers got them, and even the Mikado made copies available for his Japanese army. Today, millions of copies of this little classic have been printed, and when the author and his wife perished on the *Lusitania* in 1915 during World War I, Hubbard's reputation hinged more on this one little story than on all the other pieces he had ever penned. Paraphrased here is a brief part of *A Message to Garcia:*

When war erupted between Spain and the United States, it was vital that the U.S. president contact the leader of the dissidents. Garcia was somewhere in the mountains of Cuba; no one knew exactly where. Supposedly, no form of communication could reach him, but the president had to gain his support, and right away. What to do!

A member of the cabinet informed the president there was a fellow named Rowan who could find Garcia if anyone could. So, Rowan was called to the White House and presented a letter to deliver to Garcia.

Rowan did not ask, "Where is he? How do I get there? Will the trip be dangerous? Is it really that important? Are you sure you can't do it?"

The facts that Rowan hid the message in an oilskin pouch, strapped it over his chest, landed off the coast of Cuba in an open boat at night, traipsed into the jungle, and in three weeks came out on the other side of the island, having traveled through enemy country on foot, and delivered the message to Garcia, are not the point of the story. The point is this: President McKinley gave Lt. Rowan a message to deliver to General Garcia, and he delivered it! My Goodness, there's one whose likeness should be sculpted in marble! wrote Elbert Hubbard, as he went on to tell the rest of the story.

When I found this marvelous story many years ago, I asked Marjorie Atkins, my world-class secretary, to run off copies for the Oak Park staff, and when they returned from their summer hiatus to gather in the library, everyone read it. Our mission was to enable every student, before graduating, to deliver the message to Garcia! And, in a school that practices STAR Theory, all successful teachers, not only deliver the message to Garcia, they teach responsibility to students in such ways that students assume the proper initiative to do the same.

Each year following the one in which teachers read that riveting story, we gave every staffer the story with the same charge: Teach proper student responsibility first, and relevant subject matter follows naturally.

A few years later, toward the end of the summer, students from a neighboring school came visiting one night and painted our beautiful entrance sign in their colors. When our teachers returned, Dan Duane, who taught industrial technology, asked about the sign. I told him that I'd been trying to get it fixed. The next morning when I arrived, the sign looked like new, and I began inquiring among the staff about who was responsible. Someone said, "Drop by the wood shop and talk with Dan Duane."

I did, and Dan told me he had called some of his advanced wood students who came up that evening and did the repair work under his direction.

At the end of the week at our final staff meeting before the Labor Day weekend, I called Dan to the front of the meeting room and presented him with a miniature oak log with an axe in it. On the bottom were the words I read to Dan and the staff to close the meeting so we could enjoy the holiday before the students returned for the new school year the following Tuesday: First, I told everyone what had happened just before they returned for the pre-school workshop and then, I related the initiative Dan and his students had taken without being asked. Last, I read from the oak log, "To Dan Duane, Who Delivered 'The Message to Garcia.' " His peers gave Dan a standing ovation, sending everyone home for the holiday in great spirits.

That was the first of many "Message to Garcia" awards to staff members, students, parents of students, and friends of Oak Park High. In fact, I ran out of oak logs and axes (I started with a hundred), and the originator of the idea, Ken Bell, a former Oak Park teacher and the most creative pedagogue I have known, came to the rescue. The company didn't make the logs any longer, but had the little axes, so Ken cut another hundred logs himself, and we had more than enough to get me to retirement. The logs that remained after my departure were snatched up (with permission, of course) by super debate and forensics teacher Richard Rice who used them as awards in his nationally recognized program.

Small Schools

Many are going to find difficulty in accepting the idea of making small schools out of large ones for at least a couple of reasons. First, they say the activity program suffers. Not true. A higher percentage of students takes part in activities in small schools than in large ones, and when one finds several schools in a building that formerly housed one large school, as I have suggested doing in such cases, the public gets more for its money in building use. Scheduling activities requires cooperation, but it can be accomplished.

What many do not like is the smaller number of students that coaches and sponsors have to choose from their teams and musical groups. However, when one counts the number of youngsters participating in these programs in several schools housed in a large edifice contrasted with the number participating when just one large student body occupied the facility, one finds many more youngsters taking part, and is that not the purpose of activities: Attract as many students to the various programs as is possible?

Another reason is exemplified by what happened when Lawrence (Kansas) High School split into two high schools a few years ago. When there was only one high school in Lawrence, it dominated the other large Kansas schools in football for almost half a century, winning myriad state championships. Since it has been divided into two high schools, neither school has dominated; in fact, neither one has had many winning records since the breakup. Admittedly, this is difficult for quite a number in a community, but the citizens there and in many other places have had to choose between quality for a few and quality for many when considering the overall educational program.

I am not naive, and I realize this suggestion simply won't be acceptable in some communities and districts. Therefore, I suggest that if school people do not wish to break up large schools into small ones in the same building, there is another option if it is carefully implemented:

Take a school of eight hundred students in a modest-size community and institute the school-within-a-school idea I mentioned in an earlier chapter. There is still one school of eight hundred, but to enhance opportunities for virtually all students to exit at least competent in relevant subject matter and responsible in citizenship, organize two entities (schools) within the one school. Each of the two has its own staff and students in the basic subjects, but there is only one activity program, one school name. To succeed, however, each school-within-a-school has an identity like the Black Panthers and the Gold Panthers if the school epithet is Panthers and the colors are black and gold.

Also, each entity has a leader (associate principal, for instance, or a part-time successful teacher) who is in charge of the staff, students, and programs within that minischool. Most important though, the leader has the minischool's own community (parents, other family members, and the patrons who reside in that minischool's boundaries) to work with in building participation in and support of the school and district missions, key to the success of the minischool's students. If the district and school missions are synonymous, like, "The Hightown Schools attract and support successful teachers to improve the quality of life of all its students," then everyone continues to work together to realize that mission.

One Hundred Graduates per School?

As I wrote earlier in the book, Deborah Meier, formerly of Central Park East Elementary and Secondary School, believes that no more than about eighty graduates are optimal. Central Park East is located in the highest poverty area in New York City, yet 90 percent go on to college each year (Meier 1995). Again, if you have not read her book and are interested in quality, read it soon.

I have recommended that no more than about one hundred seniors graduate each year from a high school. The difficulty in communicating with parents and guardians, the prohibitive task of communicating with one another in school units larger than a few hundred, are obstacles too great to realize the thesis of this book. Here it is again: *Sound in pedagogy, the successful teacher creates and maintains a caring relationship with all students, rejects their acts and expressions of irresponsibility, and teaches them responsibility. Ultimately, almost all, if not all, the successful teacher's charges exit competent or better in relevant subject matter and responsible in citizenship.*

Not many parents reject that thesis. In fact, I do not know a single parent who wants less for her or his progeny. Do you? So, if we want our youngsters to exit school the way the thesis reads, we must have a preponderance of successful teachers in a school district. To accomplish this, we must communicate the needs for attracting, inservicing, and holding onto them, for they are the STARs, and only STARs in abundance, with the continuing support of those in the school community, are able to realize the thesis. On the first page of chapter 1, I said that teaching is a social science, and in social science it is far more difficult to predict success than it is in physical science. We can, however, if—with the other conditions met—we control the variable of school unit size. By making each small enough, we are able to work closely with those inside the school unit, and in the attendance area. Communication precedes support, and if the unit is too large, it is prohibitive to communicate with everyone to elicit ideas and to gain support.

Naivete?

Is it naive to believe that one of the first steps in creating successful students is reducing the number of graduates per school to about a hundred? No. It is naive to expect that in large schools virtually all exit at least competent in relevant subject matter and responsible in citizenship. It has not happened, and yet we continue to say and write that every student can and will learn. Thus, the question becomes, How small does a school unit need to be before educators have a chance to exit almost all, if not all, their students the way the thesis of this book reads?

No one really knows, but America has a case study of success in a high poverty area. So, let us try it elsewhere. It will not work, however, unless those youngsters who begin school one place continue through the senior year of high school in a district committed to achieving the same things.

I have cited three geniuses in this treatise, two theoretical, and one practical: William Glasser, who continues his efforts to persuade educators to create quality schools; Jane Nelsen, who has created a partial formula for success with her *Positive Discipline* because good discipline precedes meaningful learning; and Deborah Meier, who has helped our nation's largest city conscript enough believers to clone the enormous success of her Central Park East.

What does it take? The implementation of these four ideas: Glasser's *Choice Theory,* Nelsen's *Positive Discipline*, Meier's school smallness, described succinctly in *The Power of Their Ideas*, and STAR Theory by satisfying its assumptions as described in this book. Then, school districts have an opportunity to accomplish what many have given only lip service to the last decade: Virtually all, if not all, students graduate from school competent or better in relevant subject matter and responsible in citizenship.

I amplify and reiterate: It takes a definite plan with the components outlined to achieve what decent folks want for America's youngsters: A minimum of academic competence and citizenship responsibility for virtually all, if not all, who enter the doors of public and private schools. Some naysayers respond, "What about all the criminals, the mean-spirited, the ne'er-do-wells who inhabit every community?" The response is simple: When responsible citizens adopt and implement the plan outlined in this book, in time, the criminals, the mean-spirited, and the ne'er-do-wells diminish enough that they no longer are a significant denying force. Why? Because successful teachers are real, have unconditional positive regard for all their students, possess high empathy as well, and are outstanding in the art and science of teaching (pedagogy). In addition to possessing these traits and talent, they know how to develop and maintain caring relationships with all their students, reject their youngsters' acts and expressions of responsibility and teach them responsibility. A plethora of people like that in a school overwhelms the evil existing in a few youngsters as a result of uncaring homes. If this is so, then schools can be the panacea for the few things that ail our country.

Adopting major changes in the way schools have co-existed with the public, however, has never been easy. I recently read a book given to me by a friend, Yvonne Clevenger: *Endurance, Shackleton's Incredible Voyage*, by Alfred Lansing (1959). It is the amazing story of twenty-eight people from varying backgrounds who set out on a voyage to Antarctica with the mission of being the first to cross that continent. For the courage to embark on this voyage to "Ithaca," read Lansing's portrayal of real people back in 1915 and 1916; you might then wish to try it, for our voyage is so much easier than Shackleton and his crew's, and ours will affect the ages!

As I have discussed the thesis with my graduate students, colleagues, and others, almost everyone has agreed that small is good, but when youngsters get to high school, they need a curriculum that smallness does not provide. A plethora of studies has never conclusively shown that youngsters in communities too small to have the expansive curriculum of the schools in the suburbs, larger towns, and cities fare less or more successfully in life than their brethren from the suburbs, larger towns, or cities. Gus Baker had half the math and science courses I had in high school, but he still became one of the best math teachers in America.

For the schools of 800 to 1200, doubters cannot fathom cutting the student body into two or three schools within one building, which means dividing the community, also. For these fine folks, I recommend the school-within-a-school idea I alluded to earlier. Either way, do not lose sight of the goal to have all, or virtually all, students exit competent or better in relevant subject matter and responsible in citizenship. And the only way to accomplish this is to break large groups into ones small enough to involve the whole school community in creating a mission the residents support.

The real challenge, however, is building a district staff of successful teachers and convincing the community that it is vital to continue attracting and keeping these STARs. Implicit in this are several things:

1. STARs need reasonable student loads, no more than a ratio of 1:15 from kindergarten through third grade when teaching reading, figuring, writing, and speaking; 1:18 in fourth and fifth grade when teaching those same skills (most youngsters have reached the age of reason by fourth or fifth grade); a total load in middle and high school of no more than about 100 students for teachers of math, science, English, and foreign language; no more than a total load of about 120 for teachers of social studies, health, practical arts, and fine arts; no more than a total load of 150 per physical fitness teacher. In parochial schools, religion or theology classes number no more than 24 or 25.

2. STARs expect people to understand that becoming STARs requires time, talent, and dedication, so they need to have adequate compensation, a minimum of $60,000 a year as of the publication of this book, and with annual increases until they reach six figures. If this appears unreasonable, consider what the STARs are doing: They are preparing students to exit into the real world, where they do ordinary things extraordinarily well, and where some of the STARs' students eventually do extraordinary things, just as the STARs are doing every day in school as teachers. Surely, what STAR teachers do is more important to more people and to the nation than the product of gladiators in sports stadiums and arenas! And those gladiator stars make millions of dollars a year.

3. As mentors, STARs are also preparing future STARs, so they deserve perks, such as attending professional conferences regularly, time away from school to present papers to fellow professionals (as colleges and universities provide for their professors, some of whom are STARs), time away to make presentations in the school community, and in other communities to enhance the growth, knowledge, and production of pedagogy and responsible citizenship.

Before concluding that a six-figure salary and generous perks are out of line, consider what STARs are able to achieve: Because they (a) are outstanding in pedagogy, (b) create and maintain caring relationships with all their students, (c) reject student acts and expressions of irresponsibility, then (d) teach responsibility.

4. *Almost all, if not all, their students exit competent or better in relevant subject matter and responsible in citizenship.* I submit for strong consideration that such achievement by pedagogues is more than devoutly to be wished; it is the American dream of the ideal school when most, if not all, the pedagogues are STARs!

I cannot close this chapter without stressing again the importance of something most do not consider a basic as they do reading, figuring, and writing, and that is the skill of speaking convincingly and grammatically (Glasser 1993). If students develop the skill of speaking convincingly and grammatically alongside their development of citizenship responsibility, and a minimum of relevant subject matter competence, violence in the United States decreases dramatically. Guaranteed!

Arguably, but not very, the greatest speaker of the twentieth century was Martin Luther King Jr. He spoke convincingly and grammatically and was a responsible U.S. citizen. Arguably, but again not very, the greatest speaker of the nineteenth century was Abraham Lincoln. Some may argue that Daniel Webster was greater than Lincoln, but two of the most memorable speeches of the century were the Gettysburg Address and Lincoln's Second Inaugural Address. The former is one of the most recognized speeches in the world, more so even than Pericles'. Had the bullets of both King's and Lincoln's assassins missed the marks, violence would be but a shadow of its current rate. Citizens who learn to express themselves well orally are rare, and they should not be. Cooperation and collaboration are mainly the results of convincing and grammatical speaking by people who read, write, and figure well. Remember what Marilyn vos Savant, the person with the highest measured IQ in the world, said in reply to a youngster's question? "What is the greatest thing people have ever done?"

She averred, "The greatest thing people have ever done is decide to cooperate. Cooperation was the most important element in conquering smallpox, traveling to the moon, and achieving any peace that has lasted."

Here is a memorable testimony to the importance of speaking convincingly and grammatically: Two of my students in the 1950s were materially poor while growing up, one in Wichita, Kansas, the other in Cushing, Oklahoma. I was their English teacher and coach in junior college. An athletic booster in town told me at the beginning of Lafayette Norwood's first year at Arkansas City Junior College, "Coach, I wouldn't walk across the street to see a (racial word goes here) play any sport."

Later that school year, our college basketball team played in Hutchinson, Kansas, for the national championship, and after the game, the same gentleman came up to me and said, "Dan, I'd go anywhere to see Lafy play, and by the way, where'd he learn to speak like that? He's the most persuasive and articulate kid I've ever talked with."

Lafy, a junior college all-American, graduated in two years and went on to graduate from Southwestern College, just up the road a few miles, and while there, helped take them to the NAIA Basketball Tournament for the first time in almost twenty years, and he was a small college all-American at Southwestern. The town of Winfield, Kansas, was more than enamored of young Norwood.

The affable and articulate Norwood went back to Wichita after graduation to secure a teaching job, but although he was an exemplary student, it was still in the mid-1950s in southern Kansas, and they did not employ him. So, he went to work at Boeing building airplanes, and he applied every year to the Wichita Schools where he had graduated from the huge East High School after helping spark that school-boy roundball team to a state title in 1951.

Eventually, with superior oral communications skills, he convinced the personnel department that they should employ him, and they finally did put him in an elementary school position, eventually moving him to teacher and coach at the new Wichita Heights High School where he built a legendary program, culminating with the school's first state basketball championship. Several of his players have since played in the National Basketball Association.

When I presented Norwood for induction to the Southwestern College Athletic Hall of Fame a few years back, I told a sold-out audience, "Lafayette Norwood has changed the faces of three communities in Kansas: Arkansas City, Winfield, and Wichita. He was the first African American distinguished student-athlete to climb the mountains of Ark City and Winfield, and those communities have forever changed their demeanors for the better. He was the first African American teacher to distinguish himself in the classroom and on the sidelines in Wichita, and likewise, that city's level of tolerance for differences and accomplishments has forever soared to great heights. Now, you may believe Lafayette Norwood has helped change these communities with his athletic prowess and knowledge alone. You would be quite wrong, which you shall see when he rises to accept this honor. Citizen Norwood has achieved all this because he is highly literate, socially responsible for his fellow human beings, and is one of the most able oral communicators I have ever known."

The second young man was a Booker T. Washington High School all-American basketball player and scholar in 1955. They had separate and unequal education programs in many places at that time. When I successfully recruited Roosevelt T. Maynard in the spring of that year, he was single. When I went back to pick him up in August, he had married.

I asked "Sonny" why he had married with four years of college remaining, and he said something I've never forgotten. "Coach, Edna is the nicest person I've ever known; I love her, and I simply was afraid someone would steal her away from me if I didn't marry her now." I gulped and considered the case closed.

A lean, six-foot, three-inch Sonny Maynard was the leading scorer, rebounder, and an all-American as a first-year player on our team in 1955–56 that won the regular season national junior college championship. He earned similar laurels the next year before graduating from the same college Lafy did. Sonny was just as outstanding his last two years in college (on the court and in the classroom) as his first two. Like Lafy, he obtained a master's degree, and then Sonny continued his education through an educational specialist degree.

After a distinguished career as director of physical activities at the State Training School north of Winfield, Sonny later helped open Johnson County Community College where he taught, coached, and ended his career as a counselor. Sonny's baseball teams at JCCC won more than six hundred games, and JCCC inducted him into its first Athletic Hall of Fame class.

When I presented Sonny to the Southwestern College Athletic Hall of Fame, I told another packed house the story of how Sonny didn't want Edna to get away, and I also related his athletic and classroom achievements. I closed with, "In more than seventy years on this spinning planet, I have never known a nicer person than Roosevelt T. Maynard, and like Lafayette Norwood, he is unsurpassed in oral communications, as you shall now witness. Ladies and gentlemen, help me welcome to the microphone for your pleasure and mine, Mr. R. T. 'Sonny' Maynard."

When these two were in junior college (at different times), as I have already mentioned, I taught them English and coached them. However, a major point is this. Lafayette, Sonny, and the many others who traveled in my car myriad times when we played out of town, have told me and others time and again, often with laughter, about the value of the dialogues we enjoyed on these trips. We talked almost ceaselessly although I provided napping times for them on the longer trips, too; I corrected their English; suggested better, more concise ways to express ideas; and had geography contests (quite legal) for pennies, nickels, and dimes, which I gave the winners.

I am convinced that dialogue and collaboration are the best ways to teach many things—especially speaking, learning, and thinking skills. A requirement, however, is developing mutually caring relationships with students first so that they accept suggestions. And something else, too: Be certain that students realize you, the teacher, want to grow, also; thus, encourage them to help you grow by making suggestions. This is compatible with what I wrote in an earlier chapter about sharing your teaching mission with students and asking them to let you know when and if you are not living up to it.

In the beginning and at the end in schooling, teachers are the STARs, but they grow brighter by helping their students grow in all the right ways and by receiving unswerving support from their leaders and from those who live in the school communities.

CONCLUSION

Let's face it; unless we shoot for a plethora of STARs in our schools, and unless we do what is required to keep the STARs in place shining brighter and brighter, schools will remain as they always have been, a reflection of the nation in which they exist. However, if we attract and keep enough STARs by following the prescription in this book, our nation still receives what it deserves. The difference, however, is that the nation then gets and deserves the quality it has yearned for. Why? Because with the latter, the citizens will have worked together to help create and become a part of that quality. Maybe, just maybe, we can make our freckled schools into beautiful coats of tan!

CHAPTER 15

The Final "Necessary"

The final "necessary" (independent study services) offers a way to complete the dream of virtually all, if not all, students exiting school competent or better in relevant subject matter and responsible in citizenship. Some students simply slip through the cracks if we do not provide extra services for them, as we have for quite a few years, and as we should continue to do, for our precious special education youngsters. Independent study services are for two types of youngsters: Those who do not master the material and need more help to reach at least competence, and those who want a challenge to do extraordinary things extraordinarily well.

Both types of students might be as young as five, or as old as they are during the final year of high school. If an elementary school has a gifted and talented program, that program serves the students in one of the categories referred to above, the ones who desire challenges to do ordinary and extraordinary things exceptionally well. However, at least one other teacher in the school is designated to assist youngsters who, for whatever reason, are not making it to subject matter competence in one or more of the fundamental areas of figuring, writing, reading, and speaking at their current levels. It is essential that no youngster go to middle or junior high without figuring, writing, reading, and speaking at least at the grade level immediately preceding entry to middle or junior high. Too many enter the middle or junior high years now without proper knowledge and skills, and this is one of our failings, not just in schools, but in the homes of our children. If a longer time in elementary, middle, junior, or senior high school is necessary, regardless of research results about retention, it is a miscarriage of educational justice to pass a youngster on who is not ready to do the next level of work in the four fundamental areas. How can anyone argue that with a straight face? Consider, for instance, being a student in middle school without the knowledge and skills to perform long division. Worse yet, consider not having the knowledge and skills to perform simpler numbers functions, or not having the skills to read and understand the textbooks for that grade. It is unconscionable to allow this! Yet, we do.

If the elementary school does not have a gifted and talented program, either crank one up or develop challenging one-to-one teaching programs before or after school for these students. Pay gifted teachers stipends to develop the courses of study and to teach them. And please be certain the teachers are gifted. The same applies to the middle and junior high. High schools do not need gifted and talented programs if their subject matter offerings are rich enough.

If the middle or junior high does not have a gifted and talented program, the same applies here as in the elementary school. Additionally, at least one teacher is designated to teach those who for whatever reasons, are not mastering the figuring, writing, reading, and speaking skills necessary at their current grade levels. Again, no student exits middle or junior high without the necessary skills (already mentioned) to enter the next level, high school.

Each grade level needs a curriculum guide specifically describing the knowledge and skills necessary for competence, and describing the extraordinary knowledge and skills beyond competence in at least the four fundamental areas. Success, happiness, and a civil adult society depend on virtually every youngster acquiring at least competence in those areas through high school graduation, and beyond, if feasible. Verify this statement by studying the country's prison population. A high percentage is illiterate in reading, writing, and figuring.

I refer readers to an article I wrote in 1982, "A Recipe for Principals Who Like to Teach." One of my best school leader decisions occurred in 1959 during my first year as a high school principal in a small Kansas town, Arkansas City. A senior lacked only a half credit of English to graduate, and the counselor (we had one for 550 students) asked me shortly after the school year began if I could help the student because he needed every credit he was taking, plus another half credit in English, and he had no study hall.

I excitedly said, "Yes," and the game was on. My instructions to him were to work one unit of the English course at a time then make an appointment for the unit test. Halfway through, I had him write an essay of five paragraphs to see if he could apply what he was learning in grammar to his writing skills. I did the same when he finished the book. However, before allowing him to begin anything else, I required a pre-course five-paragraph essay without any instruction. During the next few weeks, I taught this senior the structure of a five-paragraph essay (thesis, intro, body, and closing paragraphs). Why? Because I believed, and still do, that the orderly thinking processes one learns in writing short essays carry over to orderly thinking life skills, such as on a job, in daily conversations, in understanding the daily newspaper, and in watching television programs. It goes back to Francis Bacon's assertion that reading makes the full person, conversation the ready person, and writing the exact person. The senior finished the book and the writing requirements successfully well before the first semester ended. By the way, the differences between his essay writing skills before he began and at the end were rather remarkable. Maturation, of course, might have accounted for some of the improvement, but I am certain one-to-one teaching accounted for a little, also. At that time, this 33-year-old wondered why we made students repeat whole semester courses when they needed to master only a few of the course's fundamentals valuable to them in life.

Oh yes, my first independent study English student made and kept appointments to see me, and the appointments were either before or after school for as short a time as twenty-five minutes (a unit test from the programmed grammar) to as long as an hour. I saw him no more than two or three times a week. Our developing friendship was the highlight of the course, we agreed jointly, and we continue to write one another more than forty years later. He graduated with his class in 1960, went on to community college across the street, and is still living and working in Ark City, Kansas.

In the ensuing years, I developed several independent study courses in English, and finally dropped the programmed grammar as a text. A better programmed writing text came out, one I referred to in the 1982 *Bulletin* article. The most popular independent study program, however, was one I developed with my students reading novels. They chose the books from a list of novels I had read; they read them; I tested with factual questions, and required each student to scribe a short essay explaining the thesis of the novel and describing a character I named.

At the other end, in 1966 at Oak Park High School, three teachers and I began an independent study English program for gifted students. I had six, and each of the teachers had three or four students. We chose books that all our students read; for instance, *Ship of Fools* and *Turn of the Screw*. After reading each book, students and mentors wrote critical essays. We evaluated one another's essays without knowing who wrote them. About once a month, we gathered on a Sunday afternoon in the school library for a social get-together and to discuss the independent study course they were taking. Years later, one of these students, who became a writer, wrote a biography about Harry Truman and gave me a copy with a letter, which said, in part:

> Dear Dan,
>
> Soon after opening OPHS you started an independent study course . . . and I was invited to participate. I then had doubts about being able to study books on my own, but now, almost twenty years later, I've *written* one on my own. . . . I want you to have one for two reasons.
>
> First, from the viewpoint of a male teenager, I thought you were a great principal. You understood and liked kids, and thereby believed in the future. You deserve tremendous credit for this.
>
> Second, you understood that different students had different talents. High school is one of my least pleasant memories. Then (and now) I was shy and physically weak, the classic nerd. Among my classmates, brains counted for little. Yet, as demonstrated by your independent study course, you sought to give us nerds a chance to show our talents. You encouraged us to hone what we were good at, and showed that you thought it was important. That meant an awful lot to me.

Richard L. Miller went on to say several more important things about individuality before signing off, things that support the need for all schools to offer independent study courses for the "nerds" of our schools who are not necessarily part of the "in" crowd. Richard's book, by the way, *Truman: The Rise to Power*, is an excellent treatise on the only president in this century who did not have a college education, but who was probably one of the brightest of all our presidents. Did you know Truman had read every book in the Independence, Missouri, library by the time he graduated from high school?

Thank you, Richard, for providing more than an exclamation point to this chapter. As an historian and writer, you are a great example of many students who might walk in the shadows of our classrooms and hallways, but who make extraordinary contributions to the American way of life.

Here's a story about another youngster who has no doubt found his niche as an adult. One year, Dorothy Smith, the best and most perceptive librarian I have known (other than my mother and brother) told me there was a senior who was quite bright, liked Steinbeck novels, but needed some English credit to graduate. I made him the school's Steinbeck scholar and put him to work reading the author's novels he had not yet read. He wrote a critical essay on each, and long before graduation, he had satisfied the English deficiency. Logan Stevens was a highly creative writer.

In an earlier year and time at Lawrence (Kansas) High School, I announced in a senior meeting at year's beginning that if anyone did not have room in her/his schedule for senior English and was planning to attend college the next year, I'd be happy to take that student in my "How to Write a College Essay" independent study one-half credit course. From that time on, I had at least two or three students a year work with me on an appointment basis. Lucille Vaughan Payne's wonderful paperback, *The Lively Art of Writing,* was the text, which I eventually took with me to Oak Park where one of the most successful teachers I've employed and a far better pedagogue than I, Linda Alverson, used the book in a one-semester advanced composition course we added to the curriculum for college-bound seniors. However, every year a few did not seem to fit it or college credit English into their schedules, so I eventually served them as an independent study pedagogue preparing each to write college essays.

In retrospect, the most enjoyable experiences of my educational career have been teaching one-to-one. Some reasons, although obvious, are worth recounting here to encourage teachers, school and district leaders, and parents who have not tried subject matter teaching in this mode. First, the teacher and student develop caring and often, lasting relationships unmatched in most classroom relationships. Second, because of these relationships, students are not hesitant to ask questions about subject matter that confuses them; thus, the teacher goes into depth and detail, lessening the confusion. Third, in a one-to-one independent study course, students learn much more about themselves than in a classroom: Takes or does not take the initiative to make the appointment; keeps it or does not; does the work assigned in a timely manner, or time disappears as does the learning and credit. Of the hundreds of students I have signed up for independent study English, students who need the credit to graduate, probably no more than 60 percent persevered to successful course completion. I have always said when they sign up that I do not pester them to make and keep appointments. They have the course requirements, know when they must have the work done to receive credit by graduation day, and do not hear from me until they make and keep appointments.

In elementary/middle schools, this is not the case. Teachers/school leaders ensure that independent study students are accountable at those levels. One more valuable reason for school leaders (including the STARs) to do this: Although I have helped many college-bound youngsters in independent study pursuits, most have been those who need the credit to graduate. These students, even if they do not complete the work, become your champions while they are in school and years later. Also, they get into less mischief than they would have without the incentive to graduate. Whereas most students looking back at school days remember the principal as a disciplinarian, when a principal or a teacher develops a one-to-one independent study subject matter relationship with a youngster who has historically had trouble achieving in school, guess what that student tells friends when the principal walks by in the hall, in the lunchroom, or in the mall? First, when you see him/her, you stop and visit, but the magic occurs when you walk away.

"So long, DK. See you tomorrow right after school" (if that's when the next appointment is). Then when you are not quite out of earshot, s/he starts talking with friends again. "That man's a cool dude. I wouldn't be graduating without him."

Each time I came back from retirement to lead a school, parents of some students in that school were my former students. Many were my former independent study students I had helped graduate. I remember one youngster coming up to me one day in the cafeteria and saying, "DK, Mom said you're the reason she graduated."

Another brought me a baseball cap one day in the lunchroom and said, "Dad said to give this to you, DK. He also said to tell you the DK on the front stands for Dan Kahler, not for Diamond Kings." I accepted the cap gladly and wore it as the buses arrived and departed daily.

At my last interim principalship, I was evaluating instruction in a classroom one day when my secretary sent an office helper with a note that read, "DK, please come right away to the office. We have an irate parent who won't talk with anyone but you." Needless to say, I immediately shut down my laptop and headed back to the office, a five-minute walk in the rain without an umbrella.

When I arrived and went into my office where the parent was sitting, I discovered it was one of my former students I had helped many years ago. She got up and apologized for my getting wet but immediately went into a monologue something like, "Dan, I knew you could solve this problem with my daughter because I wouldn't have graduated from high school if you hadn't solved my problem then."

She then told me about a small, solvable problem her daughter had.

The daughter was an *A* and *B* student, by the way. We spent a few minutes discussing a solution after which she said, "I knew you could figure it out!" Then she was on her way and I was fairly dry again.

CONCLUSION

The major points as I close are that (1) the school and the home work together to help virtually all, if not all, students do ordinary things extraordinarily well, and they produce some extraordinary students who achieve at higher-level cognition extraordinarily well; (2) schools are small, so cooperation becomes a habit resulting from school and home members feeling like next-door neighbors who visit across the fence; (3) these small schools have a plethora of STARs (successful teachers) who teach those en route to success in school and in adult lives; (4) home members view successful teachers as student advocates doing everything within their powers to help all students grow to at least competency in relevant subject matter and to responsibility in citizenship; (5) the word *punishment* disappears eventually, and the resulting *natural/logical consequences* become the norm in school, as these words need to be everywhere.

America is the greatest nation in the world now, but it shall be even greater when STAR Theory comes to pass. Our citizenry then rises to heights only dreamed of as crime plummets to an all-time low in a significantly safer and more productive society, for even the best can be improved. Otherwise, what is a Heaven for?

.

Beyond the Basics

Mother was a prolific letter writer. She wrote me every day I was in the U.S. Navy, including the time I was in the South Pacific during World War II. Many of those letters came in batches when we arrived in different ports. She continued writing letters to family members often until Dad passed away when he was 84 and Mother was 80. Her letters were long, yet she always used the sides of the pages before closing because she still had something to say. One of those sides always had her final words, prefaced by a P.S. I remember her postscripts as some of the most interesting and important things in her epistles. I close this, my first book, with a postscript because I have something important left to say that does not fit elsewhere.

Most folks today, it seems, are interested in improving students' reading, figuring, and writing skills, and they believe our schools are responsible for doing this. That is why this book is about those and speaking skills and not much about other important and vital areas. Public schools ordinarily offer subjects in eight areas of human knowledge and skills—language arts, science, mathematics, social studies, practical arts, fine arts, languages of other countries, and physical fitness. Church schools add courses in theology or religion.

If youngsters today began and continued with only a subject diet of reading, figuring, writing, and speaking in school, most would go mad before exiting twelve or thirteen years later. In fact, they would leave long before that. During my fifty years of working in schools, I have known several thousand students who have honed one or more of these fundamental skills only after finding their niches in other areas of human knowledge. Every school has teachers who save such students from making big mistakes—quitting school—and who enrich the lives of countless others well beyond the basics. Each reader could place an all-star cast of successful teachers in place of the cast I shall cite shortly, and I encourage you to do so.

It is important in a STAR Theory school district to realize that the accent is not only on STARs who teach reading, writing, figuring, and speaking, but on all the STARs who teach the other areas of human knowledge and skills. All are vital to the truly educated person, and parents desire a well-rounded education for their progeny. The late Norman Cousins wrote, perhaps in the *Saturday Review of Literature* that he edited for many years, something like the following, as I remember:

> A truly educated person is one who has reasonable knowledge, if not command, of the environs, who performs those acts relevant to her well-being and the well-being of those around her, who is able to think about and to anticipate the effects of causes, and who can help control the effects by helping to deal adequately with the causes. But, however impressive one's acquisition of worldly knowledge, however proficient her ability to marry theory to technique, if she cannot or does not use her thinking ability and skills to work for a safer and better world, her education is incomplete, and she is in trouble.

There my friends, is a brief treatise against which to measure a school's curriculum. Please notice that there is more than science, mathematics, social studies, and language arts implied in Cousins' description of an educated person. So, as you study the short list of STARs below, keep in mind their importance and the importance of thousands like them:

Jeanne Lawing taught art and English when Oak Park opened in 1965. The following year, she was one of the few volunteer teachers I alluded to in the last chapter who taught several independent study students English in addition to teaching a full load of art students. Jeanne, retired now, was an amazing, brilliant, and disarming pedagogue, willing to try about anything educationally sound if students were interested. I remember her standing in front of a classroom of students enrolled in her English class in 1965. She held an art object in her hand, explaining the geometry of the object and its close relationship to writing skills. The students and I were spellbound, and before departing, I was privileged to observe her turned-on youngsters begin writing an essay.

Eventually, Jeanne moved downstairs full-time to teach art, and she taught it with a passion, but with a passion that relaxed her students and unleashed in them a love of producing beautiful two-dimensional art work that seemed to jump off the canvas and into the viewers' eyes and minds. At least half her students were average in reading, writing, and figuring pursuits when they arrived in her presence in Room 145, but they left more highly literate in those fundamental areas because Jeanne Lawing elicited excellence like that from them. Occasionally, her room was also my haven from the madding crowd. Successful teachers have powerful effects on most people. They instruct you, bring out the best in you, and relax you, all at the same time. Jeanne Lawing was one of these.

Walt Graves at Winnetonka High had a similar effect. He taught beginning and advanced wood courses, and I spent more time in his shop than in my office when the troops were present. He knew his subject forward and backward, could practice what he preached, and taught as effectively as he knew and practiced it. No student was ever too much for him even though he'd use a wry sense of humor complaining about a few to relieve the inevitable pressure great teachers feel. His students honed their figuring skills in his classes because he expected everyone to figure board feet, to measure twice and cut once, to plan exactly what they needed before starting a project, and so on. I still smell the wonderful aroma of wood in his room. Walt was a treasure.

Jim Willis at North Kansas City High School was a master wood carver as well as a skilled cabinetmaker. Students loved to watch him demonstrate his figuring skills then feast on the treat of observing him do some creating. Whether the youngsters were beginners or advanced, he never was in the shop office while they were his responsibility. He was among them, teaching, empowering every one. He made them do well by way of his courtly presence and actions. Successful pedagogues do that all the time.

Clyde Welch, named Industrial Arts Teacher of the Year in Missouri during the 1970s, was chair of the department at Oak Park until his retirement. He taught drafting I, II, III, and IV, and he made certain his students not only drew straight and accurate lines on their drafting papers, they also wrote literate and correct essays periodically. Clyde Welch taught me that drafting is the language of industrial arts. I had never thought about that until he began teaching me and his thousands of students relevant subject matter in ways that made the matter stick.

Switching back to the fine arts, Bill Grace replaced an irreplaceable teacher at Oak Park after four years. I thought there would never be another Joyce Stuermer in vocal music. I was wrong. Those two pedagogues have never uttered an unkind word about a student or another human being in my presence. Wish I could say the same about myself. Joyce wrote the school and fight songs when we opened in 1965, but for years she had me and the students believing they did it. She's bound to play the lyre in Heaven and she'll play it with grace.

I'm not referring to Bill Grace, however. Bill also was the public address person at Oak Park's home football games. Had he opted for a play-by-play career on radio or television, he'd have become wealthy. His wealth, though, became much more important in a different way, as a music man every other music teacher I've met wants to emulate. The kids loved the Bald Igle (his epithet), and they won about every contest they entered, so he made them work for greatness without knowing they were really working. The Bald Igle and Joyce's (the four years before him) musicals along with the spring art shows were the events I most looked forward to every one of my twenty-one years at the school. Hundreds took part, and most had to read, write, and figure during the many weeks of preparation and a few after it was over. Those skills are vital in selling a product—in that case, the musical and art show that several thousand enjoyed each year from their comfortable seats in the Main Theatre and in the halls around it where the artworks were displayed. I've often said that a high school's fine arts department is one of the school's most important public relations ambassadors. It certainly was at Oak Park.

Another great music teacher was Barbara Hale. She made the Oak Park orchestra bold and beautiful. She played about any instrument, but her strong suit was teaching youngsters to practice often so that they could reach their best, and they did, performing in front of the music educators at the annual state convention. Barbara's husband, Glen, was the instrumental music teacher at one of our middle schools, and he was outstanding, too. What a pair of pedagogues! Together, they produced thousands of outstanding musicians who read music well, and some who wrote music just as well.

I could not leave music, however, without commenting on Gentleman Jim Chandler who made his transition recently after 85 years on this planet. He was Oak Park's first instrumental music teacher, and this former U.S. Navy Band man taught both band and orchestra. Pat White, another outstanding pedagogue who followed Jim years later, but had only the band (that's plenty, of course) to teach by that time, read at a memorial service something I had written Jim's family when

Jim passed on. Let a paragraph of the message tell a little about a great teacher:

> Dear Marie, Bill, Dick, and Jim's many loved ones,
>
> Gentleman Jim, many others, and I helped give birth to a new school in 1965, and in my eyes, he became one of the greatest educators and humans I have known. Jim possessed a serenity no other teacher approached, and this serenity made him a joy to be around. He also produced myriad quality musicians and groups of musicians, yet I never heard him say a disparaging word about anyone. Jim was loyal, diligent, kind, caring, and more than competent—he was quality through and through. I've not known another like him. Gentleman Jim Chandler is a Hall of Famer in every hall I know.
>
> > With robust love,
> > Dan & Violet Kahler

I have referred to this next teacher as the greatest debate coach in American high schools. Richard Rice came to Oak Park from a small town, Marshall, in central Missouri. He made believers of every student and parent who crossed his path. Before his first year at Oak Park ended, he had enlisted more than 100 students in his program for the following school year. His numbers grew to twice that before he moved to an associate's position in the principalship, and just a few years ago to director of staff development for the district. While he, Bill Grace, Barbara Hale, and Jeanne Lawing were at Oak Park, no high school in America had a more effective public relations department than those four. The excellence these top-notch teachers elicited from their students was known and respected far beyond district boundaries. Their students and the parents raved about them nonstop.

Mary Olshefski is a teacher of special youngsters at North Kansas City High. The year I was there as an interim principal, I was probably in her room at least a hundred times, some of which she did not see me because she was so busy helping her youngsters. They were seemingly always on task learning something that would make their lives richer then and later as adults. She always had control of the classroom, but her students loved being there because they never felt controlled. We gave an NKCHS letter to one of them, Joe McGuire, because he won a national championship in special competition back East the summer before I arrived. Track coach Ed Jackson, a consummate history teacher, presented it to him at an all-school assembly.

I have mentioned a few specifics here about only a small number of successful teachers in areas other than reading, writing, and figuring subjects. I could go on and on in each of the eight areas of human knowledge, but that must wait for another book. I'll close with one more, a physical fitness educator who also coached football and track. He no doubt disagrees with my limiting graduating classes to about 100 students, but ironically, he graduated from a small high school where he excelled athletically and academically. Gerald Crews is one of the five greatest educator-coaches I have worked closely with during my life. When we opened Oak Park, Jerry taught sociology, U.S. history, and health, and coached football and track. From the school's inception, it was apparent that young Crews (in his late twenties) was an exceptional teacher and coach. After six years when our outstanding head football mentor departed for college pastures, I appointed Jerry head coach. He was already the head track mentor by that time. His students and players idolized him, and fellow educators respected him as a teacher as well as a coach, which is a key. Coach Crews' students were successful in the classroom, and his teams were traditionally among the best in Missouri.

No man dressed as sharply as Jerry, and even in his coach's garb, he could make it into *Gentleman's Quarterly*. I cannot begin to tell you all the things youngsters, grads, parents, and his peers did to show respect and love for this man. I eventually made him activities coordinator, and he closed his esteemed career in that position and as the school's golf coach (he was a 5 handicap player).

In this postscript, you have read about just a few of the many STARs I have worked closely with, ones who did not teach readin', writin', and 'rithmetic courses. All eight areas of human knowledge belong in public schools, however, because some of America's greatest pedagogues reside there and not only teach the devil out of youngsters, they increase students' knowledge and skills in valuable areas and do it for their students' lifetimes. I estimate that if a school district dropped any one of the areas of practical arts, fine arts, physical fitness, or foreign language from the curriculum, or dropped activities from the school program, many more students would drop out or transfer. I have often said when talking to and with different audiences that without the arts, human beings go mad. I also have advised many student audiences to begin each day reading the funny papers at breakfast because those readers tend to go to school Monday through Friday, and other places on weekends with smiles instead of scowls and with pacified instead of growling tummies.

References

Ames, Carole A. "Motivation: What Teachers Need to Know." *Teachers College Record* 91, no. 3 (1990): 409–21.

Bloom, Benjamin S., M. Engelhart, E. Furst, W. Hill, and D. Krathwohl. *Taxonomy of Educational Objectives: Cognitive Domain.* New York: Longman, 1956.

Brophy, Jere. "On Motivating Students." Occasional Paper No. 101. Institute for Research on Teaching, Michigan State University, October 1986.

Brophy, Jere. "Synthesis of Research on Strategies for Motivating Students to Learn." *Educational Leadership* (October 1987): 40–48.

Cavafy, Constantine P. "Ithaca." In *The Complete Poems of Cavafy,* translated by Rae Dalven. Chicago: Harcourt, 1976.

Condry, J., and J. Chambers. "Intrinsic Motivation and the Process of Learning." In *The Hidden Costs of Reward*, edited by M. R. Lepper and D. Green. Hillsdale, N.J.: Erlbaum, 1978, 61–84.

Covey, Stephen. *The 7 Habits of Highly Successful People.* New York: Simon & Schuster, 1989.

Deming, W. Edwards. *Out of the Crisis.* Cambridge, Mass.: MIT Center for Advanced Engineering Study, 1986.

Emerson, Ralph W. "Self-Reliance." In *The Romantic Triumph: American Literature from 1830 to 1860,* edited by Tremaine McDowell. New York: Macmillan, 1949.

Gardner, John. N.p., n.d.

Girzone, Joseph. *Joshua: The Homecoming.* New York: Doubleday, 1999.

Glasser, William. *Reality Therapy.* New York: Harper & Row, 1965.

Glasser, William. *The Quality School.* New York: HarperCollins, 1992.

Glasser, William. *The Quality School Teacher.* New York: HarperPerennial, 1993.

Glasser, William. *Staying Together.* New York: HarperCollins, 1995.

Glasser, William. *Choice Theory.* New York: HarperCollins, 1998.

Goethe, Johann. *World View.* New York: Frederick Ungar, 1963.

Griessman, B. Eugene. *The Achievement Factors*. New York: Dodd, Mead, 1987.

Hubbard, Elbert. *A Message to Garcia*. East Aurora, N.Y.: Roycrofters, 1899.

Hugo, Victor. *Les Miserables*. New York: Holt, 1908.

Jones, Laurie Beth. "A Life Mission Statement." *Bottom Line* (1 February 1997).

Kahler, Dan. "Letter to the Editor." *NASSP Bulletin*. Reston, Va.: National Association of Secondary School Principals (November 1999).

Kahler, Dan. "A Recipe for Principals Who Like to Teach." *NASSP Bulletin*. Reston, Va.: National Association of Secondary School Principals (September 1982).

Lansing, Alfred. *Endurance, Shackleton's Incredible Voyage*. New York: Carroll & Graf, 1959.

Lepper, Mark R. "Motivational Considerations in the Study of Instruction." *Cognition and Instruction* 5, no. 4 (1988): 289–309.

Lincoln, Abraham. "Second Inaugural Address," 4 March 1865. Entire text of Lincoln's address can be found at www.yale.edu/lawweb/avalon/presiden/inaug/lincoln2.htm. [accessed 5 May 2001].

Lowell, James R. N.p., n.d.

Lumsden, Linda S. "Student Motivation to Learn." *ERIC Digest* 92 (June 1994): ED370200.

Maehr, Martin L., and Carol Midgley. "Enhancing Student Motivation: A Schoolwide Approach." *Educational Psychologist* 26, nos. 3 & 4 (1991): 399–427.

Maugham, W. Somerset. *The Razor's Edge*. Garden City, N.Y.: Doubleday, Doran, 1944.

Mead, Margaret. *Redbook* magazine, September 1972.

Meier, Deborah. *The Power of Their Ideas*. Boston: Beacon Press, 1995.

Nelsen, Jane. *Positive Discipline*. New York: Ballantine Books, 1987.

Nelsen, Jane. *Positive Discipline in the Classroom*. New York: Ballantine Books, 1989.

Payne, Lucile V. *The Lively Art of Writing*. Chicago: Follett, 1975.

Raffini, James. *Winners without Losers: Structures and Strategies for Increasing Student Motivation to Learn*. Boston: Allyn & Bacon, 1993.

Rogers, Carl. *Freedom to Learn*. Columbus, Ohio: Merrill, 1969.

Schlechty, P. C. *Schools for the 21st Century*. San Francisco: Jossey-Bass, 1990.

Stipek, Deborah. *Motivation to Learn: From Theory to Practice*. Upper Saddle River, N.J.: Prentice Hall, 1988.

Strunk, William Jr., and E. B. White. *The Elements of Style*. New York: Macmillan, 1959.

Swick, Kevin, ed. *Disruptive Human Behavior in the Classroom: What Research Says to the Teacher*. Washington, D.C.: National Education Association, 1980.

Tennyson, Alfred Lord. (last few lines from his poem, "Ulysses")

Williams, Marjery. *The Velveteen Rabbit*. Illustrated by Michael Green. Philadelphia: Running Press, 1981.

Vidal, Gore. *Lincoln*. New York: Random House, 1984.

vos Savant, Marilyn. "Ask Marilyn." *Parade Magazine*. April 24 and December 20, 1998. Parade Publications, 711 Third Avenue, New York, N.Y. 10017 (Reprinted with permission from *Parade* and Marilyn vos Savant, copyright 1994 and 1998.)

About the Author

Dan Kahler has been an English and biology teacher, football and basketball coach, and high school principal of several schools. After his retirement, he moved on to teach graduate courses at the University of Missouri, Kansas City. He has twice been called from principalship retirement to lead schools, and he was named Greater Kansas City's Outstanding Teacher in 1988.